I0474122

Evangelism in the Digital Age:

Media Case Studies
Volume One

Dan Henrich

Copyright 2012 Dan Henrich

All Rights Reserved

ISBN: 1469908301
ISBN 13: 978-1469908304

Author Bio

Dan Henrich is a mediastrategist with over 30 years of experience in developing contextual media. His passion is to strengthen and empower local media mission efforts by helping them enlarge their vision for what can be done. He often accomplishes this through hands-on training and projects. From his broad network of co-media professionals he has been able to bring the most modern and effective media expertise to onsite media projects and campaigns.

A large part of his successes have come from his ability to help small fledgling media operations join their resources together and accomplish broader and more effective mass media evangelism. Modeling and teaching the absolute necessity of careful research is the key to good long range planning – resulting in effective messages that cause life-changing decisions.

His cross-cultural experience in obtaining rights and dubbing existing programming has resulted in a much broader and more focused utilization of existing materials.

He has consulted and taught in the following countries in Africa: Kenya, Tanzania, Zimbabwe, Nigeria, Togo, Ghana, Benin, Cote d'Ivoire, and Burkino Faso. In the Middle East: Egypt and Jordan. In Asia: Thailand, Cambodia, Burma, Vietnam, Malaysia, Indonesia, The Philippines, Japan, South Korea, Peoples Republic of China, Taiwan, Hong Kong, Singapore, India and Pakistan. He has a graduate degree in Script and Screenwriting from Regent University in Virginia.

Dan has been married to Christine for over 38 years and have four children and four grandchildren. They currently reside in Southern California. His email is info@comresources.org.

Acknowledgements

I want to thank all those who contributed for this first volume of *Evangelism in the Digital Age: Media Case Studies.*

Thanks also to my reviewers and editors - Gerald Davis, Mary Sue Verhagen, Phil Cooke, Mark Snowden and John Gowan for the support and comments.

Special thanks to my wife, Christine Henrich who is my co-consultant on many of these projects and the love of my life.

Dan Henrich
Mediastrategy Consultant
http://www.comresources.org/
Email: Info@comresources.org

Contents

Introduction

Evangelism in the Digital Age: Media Case Studies is a collection of case studies on using media for evangelism and church planting.

Many of these projects are the result of my mediastrategy consulting practice so they are fresh in my mind as I compile them. Because of this, the discussion questions and lessons learned are not academic, they are the result of my involvement in developing the strategy and implementing the projects.

 Like any collection of case studies, the goal of this book is to help media mission producers and those in training to learn from others.

Dan Henrich, Communication Resources International.

Section One:
Video and Film

VIDEO/FILM CASE 1: DRAMATIC FILM

Category: Drama
Location: Kenya
(versions in English, French and Swahili)

Sabina's Encounter is a dramatic film designed to help the average African deal with the socio-cultural pressures created by a woman's barrenness.

Synopsis

In a dramatic opening, Sabina, a barren woman in her late twenties, approaches the home of her sister Maria. Sabina's husband has visited a witchdoctor who has told him Sabina is a witch and worthless, and to send her away. The husband has beaten Sabina severely and sent her away. She arrives very depressed, nearly suicidal and hating the world and God. Sabina's husband comes to tell her to have her family send the bride price back to him. There he meets Maria's wise friend Mzee Paulo, who has talked to Sabina.

During this talk, Mzee Paulo has presented the concept that the wife is not the only cause of a childless family. But Sabina is depressed and bitter, seeking Maria's peace, although she thinks Maria's answer in Christ is too simplistic.

A baby is found thrown into the pit latrine, and through this traumatic experience Sabina realizes that it is not babies, not clothes, not a husband that gives peace. During this time her sister leads her to the Lord.

Strategic Objective

1) To cause Christians to understand critical issues of their culture and how to relate to them in the Christian faith.

2) To provide information about the causes of barrenness and remove the superstition that is often associated with it.

3) To teach basic spiritual issues to new and old believers who are still young in Christian growth, that they may grow and reach out to others.

Areas of Use

Sabina's Encounter has been distributed in many countries in sub-Sahara Africa in English and more recently, Swahili and African French. More than ten countries have aired this program.

Estimated Audience

Reports received from the main cinema van distributors in

Kenya, Tanzania, and Ghana, as well as from national TV stations, indicate that more than 18 million people had viewed the film by December 2002.

How was it produced?

Sabina's Encounter was a co-production of Handclasp International, a non-profit organization (Communication Resources International) and International Media Ministries (Assemblies of God).

The initial work on the project, including the research and script preparation, was initiated by Henrich and a group of African leaders and talented writers.

The above-the-line budget was raised by CRI and International Media Ministries, who provided the below-the-line personnel and equipment through post-production and film transfer.

Script and production

The script was written by two very gifted writers from Kenya and Cameroon along with team leader Dan Henrich and was based on real life situations that exist in the African culture today.

Agreements were drawn up detailing the responsibilities of each of the co-producers which included schedules, funding, pre-production, production, and post production.

Additional strategies were laid down detailing marketing of the film/video as well as ownership of the product, language rights and escrowing of royalties for future joint productions.

Research

The writers submitted their script to a panel of 16 men and women from a variety of countries then made the necessary modifications to the original script.

The choice of characters, location and music was also very important to the overall planning of the program. In fact, all of the music was original and was very important in reinforcing the theme as well as providing strategic bridges throughout the story.

Further testing of the product was completed after it was created and critiqued, both by local people who watched it and by professionals who analyzed it for content, technique and acting. Many letters, calls, and remarks received after the projection of the film have confirmed its impact.

Many TV stations that have used it over and over again on national and regional television have made a further plea for the second in this series to be produced.

Status: The film is available in Kiswahili, African French and Kenyan English. It continues to be shown on African TV stations.

Produced in the early 1990s, by 2004 it was seen by well over 20 million people with nearly 500,000 verified decisions for Christ. Because it deals with a well-researched felt need, the film is "evergreen" and is used by many denominations both in outreach and as part of counseling sessions.

Copies can be ordered at <u>https://www.createspace.com/306525</u>

FMI: Dan Henrich - <u>info@comresources.org</u>

VIDEO/FILM CASE 2:
MOBILE CINEMA VANS

Category: Film Distribution
Location: Kenya, Tanzania, Ghana

Reaching the smaller towns and villages of Africa is not something to be taken lightly, either in advertising or in evangelism.

Mobile cinemas in Africa have been operating since colonial days under government auspices to communicate messages on health, agriculture and other social information. In later years, advertising was used to pay for the operational costs of these government vans and although there were pro-social films being used in 1989, the Kenya Film unit was showing so-called 'kung-fu' movies with local language voice overdub. This is the way audiences were reached by the advertisers of toothpaste (with free samples), cooking fat, seed and baby formula.

Kenya

In 1974 a group of missionaries associated with several missions started Afromedia Christian Production to produce alternative films for

Christian and non-Christian audiences. It produced one major film, *Checkpoint*, in addition to a sustained effort in television programming for Kenyan children. A study of Cinema Leo's Coast Circuit revealed that 55% of Muslims surveyed noted that viewing Christian cinema 'helped them live better lives,' showing that Cinema Leo has a potential impact on Muslims.

Although current data is unavailable, several years ago Cinema Leo*'s* five vans visited 26 towns and villages each month during the dry season and had a monthly viewership of 250,000 people.

Tanzania

Under the support and training of Cinema Leo, the Evangelical Lutheran Church formed the "Sinema Leo" ministry consisting of one mobile van that has a longer term impact on selected communities by visiting regularily for two years. They spend a week in each area going door to door and inviting people for the evening show*s*. These local people in the selected communities also give SL feedback about what is going on among the viewers that evening and afterwards in the village. During the other visits we are officially invited by a Pastor, Evangelist or a given Outreach Ministry. Local believers prepare people who will help with home visits during the day, and follow up after the one-week film program.

Many times the film show will include educational films produced in Africa, as well as the Swahili version of *Sabina's Encounter*. Sinema Leo has only one van and one full time evangelist.

Ghana

Challenge Enterprises (CE) of Ghana operates a cinema

van network that was started in 1980. CE now operates eight vans that show Christian films 22-26 nights of the month. Over the 25 years of the ministry, the vans have presented the Gospel to 21,000 communities, towns and villages in Ghana.

On the average, 2500 - 3000 people view these films each night per van. 3,600,000 people have made decisions to follow Christ and 162 churches have been planted in collaboration with local churches. CE also sells books and cassettes from the eight vans as well as from 18 bookstores across Ghana.

Strategic Impact

It is clear that there are ways to impact the audiences of these three cinema van networks reaching the rural people in typical African ways using media. Because of funding, these vans show American films which do not address the felt needs of the audience. Andrew Anami, Cinema Leo's General Manager, believes that African films like *Sabina's Encounter* (See Video/Film Case 1) and Afromedia's one and only *Checkpoint* film are best suited to reaching his country.

Training and Co-production

Much like *True Stories from Asia* (Video/Film Case 9 - Dramatic Short Films), media partners could come alongside these Christian ministries and help them produce short, low budget dramatic films that touch the hearts of Africans. To do this requires training and partnership in equipment and editing.

Because they use video projectors, lower level DVcam equipment is all that is necessary.

Involvement

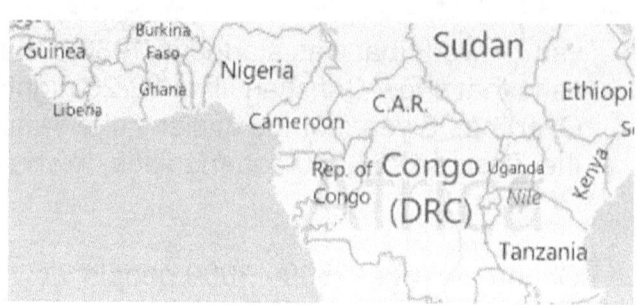

STEP ONE - Meet with the staff of the ministry and determine if they are interested in a partnership.

STEP TWO - Discuss the felt needs that touch the audience where the cinema vans go and some story ideas that fit into the agenda of your organization.

STEP THREE - Discuss a possible training program. Perhaps this will involve development of specialized modules. For example, maybe they need help with scriptwriting and editing.

STEP FOUR - Implement a series of workshops to quickly bring the production level up, equipping them to share the stories that will impact them for the Lord.

NOTE: The author has done a series of these tips-on-training partnerships and is willing to provide more detailed support.

Discussion

A partnership of this kind can overwhelm your other projects. What sort of safeguards would you set up to protect both your time and theirs to ensure professional level interaction?

FMI: Dan Henrich - info@comresources.org

VIDEO/FILM CASE 3: INDIAN MARRIAGE FILM

Category: Film
Location: India

After consulting on an existing Indian film project and determining that the script was not viable, we entered into partnership with an Indian production company to produce a theatrical release film on marriage...

Synopsis of Film

Johnny Bhai (Johnny Lever) is an amusing older married man with a heart of gold. Vijay (Sumeet Pathak) is a young man who is in love with Sneha (Neetu P Chaudhury). Vijay and Sneha get married against the advice of both Dr Sheetal, a qualified family therapist, and Johnny Bhai and immediately begin to realize that the person they thought

was perfect had flaws! Conflicts start invading their daily life. Vijay goes to Johnny Bhai but doesn't like his advice. What Vijay wants is sympathy and comfort, but he gets sage advice from this experienced married man. Sneha seeks counsel with Dr Sheetal who advises her that problems of this type are to be expected. After all, Vijay does not beat her or go out with other women - he simply ignores her and argues! Sneha should do one good thing for her husband each day for a week without expecting anything back. Sneha takes her advice and starts a one-week experiment. She asks Vijay to call his parents for dinner and she will cook for them. Vijay is surprised and happy with this offer. Of course, the dinner with Vijay's parents is a disaster but the experience brings the young couple closer together. This love story takes an interesting turn when Vijay's wealthy and beautiful boss, Jyothi (Mansi Lal) tries to seduce him. What happens next is something that will take Vijay to a point of no return…

Partner's Strategic Objective

The strategic objective was to impact unsaved Indians who were struggling with their marriages. According to public data, India has traditionally had the lowest divorce rate (1.1%) in the world. However, the trend is changing in the last few years. In 2007 the number of divorce cases filed in the Family Court of Chennai was 3874. It increased to 4643 in 2010. But the most worrisome factor is "dry marriages" - marriages that exist without love and respect. In India divorce is a social stigma that forces many married couples to live together instead of sorting out their differences. When there is a problem in marriage, couples do not opt for professional marital counseling. The woman will go to her parents for sympathy and the man will go to his parents for support. Therefore, the overall counseling they get is biased and makes things more difficult for the marriage.

Revised Strategic Objective

After consulting with the partner and working on the script together, we revised the story to include an office cell group and the reading of various *Scriptures*. For example, these Bible verses and concepts are addressed in the film.

"At the very beginning of time, God was there, and there was nothing else…only God. He spoke, and when he did, he created the universe and everything in it. Then he decided to make a special creation—man. So, God created man and woman. He had a perfect relationship with them. He walked with them, talked with them, and took care of them—until one day, the man and woman disobeyed God, and they broke their relationship with God. They were separated from God…

[4]Love is patient, love is kind. It does not envy, it does not boast, it is not proud. [5]It is not rude, it is not self-seeking, it is not easily angered, it keeps no record of wrongs. [6]Love does not delight in evil but rejoices with the truth. [7]It always protects, always trusts, always hopes, always perseveres. [8]Love never fails.

The character Johnny Bhai talks about learning the meaning of love from the Bible. Johnny models reading the Bible aloud to his wife in an amusing exchange: "Better to live on a corner of the roof than share a house with a quarrelsome wife. *A* quarrelsome wife is like a constant dripping."

Vijay states: "I thank God every day for giving her to me."

In addition to these scriptural concepts, the characters model positive roles in solving marital problems, including going to a marriage counselor.

Area of its Use (target group):

This film was produced in Tamil, but with plans to dub to Hindi and Kannada.

Estimated Audience
This project was released in two stages:
January 2011 was the audio release. A CD with all the songs was promoted and is selling in stores. In addition, a PR company was hired, 19 television stations covered the release, and the music videos are still airing on several television stations.

The Hi-res digital "print" was prepared by Qube from the 4K output of the Red Camera, and the 5.1 Dolby was completed for the June 2011 preview event.

How was it produced?

Anbirkku Alavillai was produced by Shepherd India Media Private Limited or SIMPL. SIMPL is a small Chennai-based company that produced a series of television sitcoms several years ago and distributes Christian DVDs. The director, Jim Sanjay, is the author of several books and is very creative.

There were a variety of donors. One donated

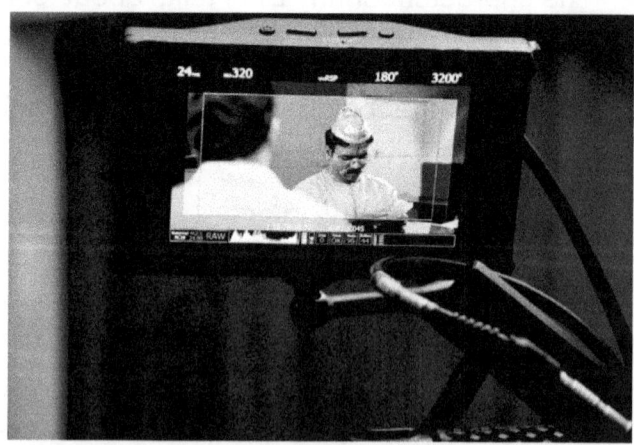

approximately 18% of the $190,000 budget to date, but the majority of funds came from within India.

Current status?

It has been difficult to attract a commercial distributor because *Anbirkku Alavillai* is categorized as a "family film" and has neither a Hindu temple scene nor crude jokes. Right now, preview shows are continuing with very positive responses from both Hindus and Muslims. Linkages are being made with Christian organizations to help with the marriage counseling requests.

We are discussing the concept of renting local theaters and finding sponsors to pay for the tickets. Several TV stations have approached the partner for rights and this is under consideration for India as are rights for companies targeting Indians in other countries, such as Tamil TV Malaysia.

If no theater distributor is found, the project will not re-coup production expenses. In late 2011 the film was shown in Punjab state in its Hindi and English version in theaters and also some of the large schools. Now, believers in other cities have requested showings with a potential to reach thousands who have never heard. All that is needed is a 6000 Lumen video projector!

FMI: Dan Henrich - info@comresources.org

VIDEO/FILM CASE 4: CONTEXTUAL DVD DISTRIBUTION

Category: Bible Stories Drama

Location: Asia

Title: Ancient Journeys

This case discusses various aspects of finding what you (as media consultant) might consider as effective and discussing this with strategy personnel.

This historical series was produced by Geolink Resources in the Middle East in the Arabic language. It consists of 15 hours of programs. Information on the series can be found on http://www.ancientjourney.com/ which is how Communication Resources International (CRI) has chosen to market the series. CRI has the Asia rights for the series.

Having received the file, I immediately started discussing it with strategy personnel in Indonesia and Malaysia. Most were interested and thought that Adam & Eve, Cain & Abel, Abraham, and the Passover would be the most important of the nine stories in the series. A leadership change and budget issues, however, created an adaptation issue so that some strategy personnel were not interested in the series, as it was not easily available to them.

We started branching out and showing the series to GCCs in Asia. These included Bangladesh, India and Malaysia.

Strategic Objective

1) To use stories familiar to high identity, low practice Muslims using contextual subtitling.

2) Depending on the Muslim's interest in Arabic (Allah's language), to develop an association factor to the materials.

3) Although the G2 producers (http://www.godsstories.ae) openly talk about the Bible in their website, we have positioned the series as *Ancient Journeys* or in Indonesian, *Human Stories* (http://www.perjalananmanusia.com/) and do not mention the Bible connection.

Distribution

Indonesia: After getting approval and funds to sub-title the films into Indonesian we realized that most personnel and other GCCs would use something that was available. Using contacts with Tarra Entertainment we entered into a contract for them to mainstream the series in their 60 company-owned stores, 3 Societie, 10 Carrefour, 20 Gramedia Bookstores, 3 Metro Department and 50 Christian bookstores. In addition, we have an agreement with 6 regional TV stations to air the series during Ramadan.

India: "Adam & Eve" has been dubbed into Tamil and we have just finished Urdu. The Tamil version was sold to a religious TV channel whose viewers are very excited.

Status

The series is available in Indonesia and India.

FMI: Dan Henrich - info@comresources.org

VIDEO/FILM CASE 5:
INDONESIA TV

Category: Television
Location: Indonesia

In an attempt to reach a large number of Indonesians on Easter Friday, a group of Christian organizations banded together to use Mel Gibson's Passion of the Christ (POTC) on national television.

The Christian Broadcasting Network (CBN) was the lead partner in this project. They had been working in partnership with Indonesian believers to raise the funds to acquire airing rights for POTC for airing twice on national television. Most of the major TV stations are owned by Christian-background people who are shy about putting overt Christian programs on their stations because they might offend the militant Muslim minority and have their property attacked. In this case, airtime was purchased on TRANS-TV, a free-to-air station available in 20 major metropolitan areas, three satellite networks and three cable systems. The Trans TV website claims 33 broadcasting sites and a potential viewership of 150 million of the 237 million population. Trans TV hits an upper middle

educated class, perhaps a C/B demographic, and at the time in 2008 project planners expected an audience of 2.4 million or 1% of the population.

In about February of 2008 a group of mission representatives met at IMPACT Indonesia to figure out how to follow up on the expected airing. CRI was approached to assist with the strategy and *to* approach a major foundation for the funding with the encouragement of C.S., a former CPer with a major mission group working in Indonesia.

CBN's SOLUCI program attracted a large number of Christians and used Christian terminology such as Yesus Christus for Jesus as opposed to Isa Al Masih, the Koran's term for Jesus. In fact, Campus Crusade has recently done a contextual Jesus film and eventually a DVD was created that would be offered as a premium to viewers. The DVD included parts of this contextual J-Film, several re-enactments of miracles, and a testimony of Miss Indonesia, a former Muslim and a former imam, now follower of Isa.

Strategy

Several times throughout the POTC offers were made to viewers that if they answered four questions correctly they would "win" a DVD. Of course, the respondents had to include mailing addresses! Respondents could also call into to CBN's help line and the Gospel was presented verbally. No data is available from CBN. Each of the people who replied was sent this DVD and a questionaire to determine the demographics of the respondents as the goal was to identify Muslim "Heads of Households." Some of these were given to a ministry called the Indonesian Peoples Network (IPN) to follow up and some to a consortium of mission groups who had committed to following them up on a face to face basis.

Report by Objectives

Here is the report sent to the foundation that provided follow-up funding:

> **GOAL**: Because the broadcast will be promoted locally by believers who will do the follow-up as well as radio broadcasts by other media ministries, we expect that well over one million will view the *Passion* nationwide.
>
> > *RESULT*: Trans TV claims to have an audience of 2.4 million people. Promotion of the broadcast was not done well, except on the Christian Broadcasting Network programming that has a dominant Christian audience.
>
> **GOAL**: 100,000 Muslims will be presented with a DVD on the Life of Christ in Contextual Bahasa Indonesian.
>
> *RESULT*: 65,000 individuals answered the text message contest correctly and "won" a contextual DVD on the Life of Christ.
>
> **GOAL**: 50,000 respondents returning the questionnaire for the 2nd DVD premium, with 5,000-7,000 fitting into the potential Muslim persons of peace (heads-of-households / influencers) demographic.
>
> *RESULT*: 17,000 individuals returned the questionnaire. Only 780 of them fit into the Muslim heads-of-household category. Of those followed up by text message, it turned out that 711 were Muslim, 47 Hindus, 19 Christians and 15 unclear.
>
> **GOAL**: 50 %, or 2500 to 3500, requesting a Shellabear printed Bible or the entire Shellabear video *Matthew*.

RESULT: 399 individual contacts were sent to the field workers for "a face to face" treatment. These contacts were adopted by several Independent Field Teams (IFT) representing both USA missionary groups and national church planting groups, and some through individuals.

GOAL: Evangelists will meet each of these souls and deliver the Gospel materials and develop a relationship with them with the goal of presenting a message of salvation and starting a house church.

RESULT: This did not actually happen. Of the individuals sent to IFT, (#4 above) feedback to the project was not as positive. Only ten people accepted Christ and the field teams reported that four of them were involved in a house church.

GOAL: Of the 2500 to 3500 contacts, we project 500 to 700 new groups and 250-350 new churches (or about half the groups becoming churches with an estimate 80% of these new churches reproducing within the first year). Each of these contacts, groups and churches will be overseen by qualified and trained Church Planters under the general oversight of the network of 20+ Indonesian CPM trainers.

RESULT: Due to the loss of a key person, the Indonesian Peoples Network (IPN) was forced to close down operations and lost final data. IPN was the operating entity that had received the Muslim contacts from the Christian Broadcasting Network(CBN). IPN and the information regarding the establishment of house churches by individuals followed up by IPN is not available.

Are the actual outcomes different from the projected outcomes?

Yes, lower than we anticipated.Which outcomes did you find easiest to measure?

Those individuals' names that were given to the IFTs as data were for the most part not followed up by those teams. Did you find that your projected outcomes were well chosen as a way to evaluate your project?
Yes. However they were unrealistic due to the lack of promotion of the program initially. How would you modify the projected outcomes in light of your actual experience?

What would you do differently next time?

Include the partners deeper in the process, whereby the follow up partners are not viewed as mere partners, but actually taking ownership of the leads they are given from the beginning.

What did you learn/gain from this experience?

1. We must lower expectations of the % of target audience responding.
2. We must involve partners not only in follow up process, but in training/educating them in process early on so when they pass on leads to their staff, is not viewed as being received from an outsider, but from an insider.

If your project is on-going, how well have your plans for long-term sustainability progressed?

We have gained one substantial national partner, who has keen interest.

Discussion Questions

1. How could this project be more effective?

2. How does the involvement of a broad variety of Christian organizations help a project like this?

3. What do you think of the discrepancies between projections and actual respondents?
4.
FMI: Dan Henrich - <u>info@comresources.org</u>

Video/Film Case 6:
Dramatic TV
Philippines

Category: Television
Location: Manila, Philippines

During holidays in the Philippines, approximately 70 of the 82 million Filipinos spent significant time with their families and some of that time watching special TV programs and movies.

Background

The Mass Media ministry of the Philippine Baptist Mission (MM-PBM) strategized that one-hour dramatic true-story movies would be an effective means of sharing the Gospel. Through convention meetings and response to the radio programs there were five or six well-known and very dramatic conversion stories of well-known Filipinos. The MM-PBM spent a few months researching and validating the

information in the stories, including face-to-face time with the story subjects, to insure accurate information for the portrayal of the person and the events related to the conversion. A

big part of the investigation was to insure that the person was still growing and living with a good Christian testimony.

Originally the Mass Media–PBM was funded by what is now the International Mission Board (IMB) to buy air time and show these on at least the two major holidays four or five times and on the two major channels. When funding for this dried up, MM-PBM was able to get the Christian Broadcasting Network 700 Club-Manila to pay to air them with the agreement that money received would go to the 700 Club and responses and questions about the Gospel to MM-PBM.

Synopsis

Kid Labrador is the story of a famous Filipino boxer who started out as a street child who was always getting into trouble with the law. As a young man he was recruited and trained to become one of the Philippines' best boxers. But he became corrupted by his fame, and the harsh lifestyle caused him to lose his title and his family. After some years with almost nothing, his life changed dramatically when a friend from his past won him to Christ!

My Life for His is the story of twin boys born into the slums of Tondo, Manila, Philippines. One grows up to become a Baptist pastor, well known throughout Manila because of his poor and difficult years in Tondo and his Christ-like ministry as an adult. The other twin was always in trouble as a child and grows up to be a common thug who eventually manages to work himself into a gang and then rises to the top as the gang leader. One night a rival gang sneaks into his mother's house to kill him. In the dark they stab him several times and he dies in his own bed.

The next day the mother comes to wake up her son and finds him brutally murdered. Except, it is the good son who had come home for a visit. The gangster son had been out all night carousing and had escaped death.

Over the next several weeks,family and neighbors and church members tell the gangster son over and over all the wonderful things his brother did and how he had changed their lives because of his life in Christ. The brother breaks down and accepts Christ. God soon calls him to step into his brother's footsteps and he takes up the mantle of his brother's pastoral ministry.

Commander King: A young boy grows up in the mix of poverty surrounded by friends and neighbors who join the New Peoples Army to fight against the capitalist corruption of Marcos and his government.

He begins enlisting the help of a shaman who gives him amulets to wear and lotions to rub on his body. The shaman tells him. "These will make you bullet-proof!" Pretty soon the young soldier boldly goes out to the front of each skirmish – not bothering to hide behind a tree to fight but stepping out in the middle of the gunfight and successfully killing his enemies while never getting a scratch. This goes on for a few years and he becomes famous all over the Philippines as Kumander King!

But eventually, his band of soldiers is ambushed and he is taken captive and put in prison. There the warden, who is a strong Christian, begins to gain a relationship with King and shares the Gospel with him over and over.

One night on his cot in his cell, King hears God speaks to him and tell him that He is the true protector, the all-powerful God able to save to the uttermost. King awakes in the morning asking to see the warden, shares his experience and gives his life to Christ.

While still in the prison he receives an invitation to join the Mass Media – PBM Bible Correspondence Course. Throughout the next several months he grows in his knowledge of God's word and his call to service. When he is released he feels called into ministry. Because of his famous career as an NPA soldier, he has many opportunities to share his testimony both in his local church and in large evangelistic crusades. He eventually settles down to pastor a small church in the town where he grew up.

Discussion Questions

1. These films seem "evergreen". Although they are too old for television, how could they be re-purposed for new media?

2. As organizations grow and change, people retire and masters are mis-placed. Should organizations take advantage of modern technology to archive programs like these films?

Edited by Dan Henrich - info@comresources.org

Video/Film Case 7:
Dubbing in Asia

Category: Distribution
Location: SouthEast Asia

A major Christian organization wants to dub some of its programs into languages that would impact your target people groups. You know that this is a high quality organization with some fine films. In this case it is in three nearby countries. You have had experience with getting programming done before in one of the countries but not the others.

What are the considerations on your part?:

1. Does this fit into my mandate to get evangelistic materials into the hands of the lost?
2. Will this require significant amounts of my time?
3. What would be the first steps?

This organization is not connected in these countries but wants you to assist them in getting the translation done, finding and vetting a quality studio and making sure the project is done professionally.

STEP ONE - Locate studios in the other two countries. Email all your contacts there to see what is available and track the studios down to see what they have done. Search the Internet for studios and start the process of getting quotes based on number of characters and duration. Networking on my part was essential as I had both Christian and secular media contacts in these countries. In the case of V and M, no Christian films had been dubbed in-country so we had to make sure the studio saw us as a business.

STEP TWO - Contract with the studio in the country in which you have experience (T) and start translation of all three languages.

STEP THREE - Get the ministry to send three sets of masters with split M&E tracks, either directly to the studios or to you for hand-carrying into the country. (We had to hand-carry materials to V and M). While you are there, investigate the studio and talk to the sound/editors.

STEP FOUR - Negotiate the contract with both the ministry (what assistance will you provide?) and the studios. This should include delivery of the final production, DVD and artwork adaptation.

Discussion Questions

1.Are the three "considerations" above the only ones or are there more?

2.Are you networked enough in even in your city to do such a project? What could you do to change that?

3.Make a list of both Christian and secular media groups you know. Now map out a way to meet the groups.

Written by Dan Henrich - info@comresources.org

VIDEO/FILM CASE 8: PROJECT VIDEO

Category: Video - Small Media
Location: SouthEast Asia

Project VIDEO is a major media initiative of Wycliffe Bible Translators in Asia that is attempting to develop dozens of video production centers and train the ethnic producers who manage them to target their own language groups in "proclaiming the Gospel through video."

Strategic Objective:

In the God's Two Carabao strategy, one carabao represents the ethnic evangelists in Asia who actually do the MINISTRY. The other carabao represents the congregations in the U.S. who consider it their MISSION to help their fellow carabao do their ministry. They do this by sponsoring one of three different PROJECT PACKAGES, which include a DVCAM camera kit, a Mac editing system, and funding to do an initial dubbing or original production. In 2011 this package required an investment of about $20,000.

Every congregation that sponsors a PROJECT PACKAGE is encouraged to send one or two service volunteers to Asia on a Project Video trip where they will:

- Catch a vision for proclaiming the Gospel through video in vernacular languages
- See and dedicate a new production center
- Meet members of the people group being targeted by this production center and worship with local believers

Area of its Use

Currently, Project Video has three production centers up and running that target three of the six Hill Tribe people groups in northern Thailand - LISU, KAREN and AKHA. LAHU will be our next target group (2011), then the HMONG (2012). Attempts will be made to distribute the gospel videos being produced in these centers to those same ethnic populations living in the neighboring countries of Burma, China, Laos and Vietnam, and to those refugees (especially the KAREN and HMONG) who have immigrated to other countries around the world. The primary target group who we hope will use and distribute our vernacular DVDs are local pastors, lay leaders and evangelists involved in church planting and discipleship ministries.

Estimated Audience

The six Hill Tribe people groups living in northern Thailand and neighboring countries total more than 10 million people.

How was it produced?

Ethnic producers make all of our productions, either by dubbing proprietary films that Project Video has the legal rights to dub:

- VISUAL BIBLE (Acts and Matthew)
- TODAY WITH GOD (John)

- NEW MEDIA BIBLE (Luke and Genesis)
- GOD PROVIDES FILM SERIES (Crown Financial
     Ministries)

or by shooting and editing their own original productions:
- talking / teaching heads
- music videos
- Biblical dramas
- etc.

The field directors and ethnic producers at each production center work with local "production committees" (consisting of local pastors, lay leaders, evangelists, etc.) in determining what productions to make each year. These committees also evaluate and approve pre-production plans and completed masters (before they're duplicated) for quality control purposes.

Current status?

LISU - have production centers in Gongshan, China (2009) and Yangoon, Burma (2011) but the field director is not consistently supporting local producers, so only four productions have been completed to date.

KAREN - will be completing a new $65,000 media center in 2011. This is our "model" ministry. Great field director. Excellent local producers (staff). Fantastic production output. Will provide the venue for the new training program that Kevin Landwer-Johan will be developing for Project VIDEO.

AKHA - audio studio has been built (in Chiang Rai, Thailand). Equipment has been delivered. Team of 3 AKHA evangelists will launch the ministry Sept. 2011 after Paul Vernon returns from furlough in the U.S. Paul will be the manager / trainer of this production center and I'm very optimistic that it will do well in the years ahead and that their ministry will impact AKHA all over Asia.

LAHU - field director (LAHU leader) and local LAHU producers have been identified. This production center will be in Chiang Mai. I'm currently promoting three PROJECT PACKAGES for this ministry.

Discussion

Historically, many mission organizations developed production facilities but the actual production was dependent on missionaries and very little training was done. As a result, when the key missionary moved, the equipment sat idle and the studio was eventually closed.

What makes this strategy different is that all actual production is in the hands of locals (field directors) and missionaries. Training is done either by neighboring centers or other Christian groups. Smaller languages are also targets, but basically PV is providing a capability for locals to actually do production targeting the lost.

Do you think this is a valid strategic approach? Why?

Could this approach be used in urban settings producing programming for mobile devices and web outreach?

If such a center were available in your area, how could you be involved in helping them become more effective?

FMI : Don Leonard VVMI@aol.com

Video/Film Case 9:
Dramatic Short Films

Category: Drama
Location: Asia
(versions in English and Thai)

True Stories from Asia consists of two short films: The Monk and Jesus *and* The Story of Oye. *The stories behind these films were told in a missions conference in Asia.*

Synopsis

The Story of Oye opens with her telling how she became a believer in Burma. She was visiting some friends and a 'sweet voice' said "Daughter, come next door." When she went there she found a circle of people studying the Bible. They invited her in and explained the way of salvation. She accepted Christ but when she told her parents, her father beat her and forbade her to associate with Christians. Eventually he reneged and she is now serving a pastor and his wife in a small mountain area of Burma.

The Monk and Jesus is about a monk who is hit by a car. The doctor tells him is injury is inoperable and they are going to amputate his leg. That night a man (Jesus) appears to him and tells him not to worry as he will heal him. That

night his leg gets warm and in the morning he is healed. No one has heard this name of Jesus and the monk goes back to the monastery. One day, two people tell him about the Living God who has a Son named Jesus. The monk says he knows this Jesus and wants to follow Him.

Strategic Objective

1) To cause Buddhists to understand that the living God can touch their lives.

2) For Buddhists to see that God is a powerful God and can work miracles in their lives

Areas of Use

This project was intended for SE Asia. It was shot in Thai with English voice overs. Eventually we would like to do a Burmese version.

Estimated Audience

Unknown

Script and production

The original stories were transcribed and a storyboard done by the director and videographer. A Thai dialogue director (Somkit) was hired to recruit actors usually employed as Likay dancers with the Christian Communicate Institute in Chiang Mai, Thailand.

Somkit located a house that would do for both films and a team of the actors, cameramen and still photogs started at 8am.

Very little lighting was used as electricity was problematic. We used reflectors as needed.

The project was edited using FCP and the two English voice overs were volunteers.

These two production were shot in one day and edited in a

week. From pre-production to posting we used about six weeks.

Budget

About $1,000 for above-the-line talent. All below-the-line costs were paid for out of other budgets.

Status

These films have been posted various places on the Internet. A Japanese version was done. Personnel of the sponsoring organization have little interest to date in mobile distribution.

Discussion Questions

1. What could have been done at the pre-production stage to ensure that these films had more distribution?

2. Have you ever worked with actors? What would you have done differently to make this more effective?

Written by Dan Henrich - info@comresources.org

VIDEO/FILM CASE 10: ADAPATION OF THE HOPE

Category: Storying Videos
Location: Asia

This case discusses various aspects of adapting THE HOPE into several languages of SE Asia.

Created in co-operation with motion picture producers and distributors around the world, The HOPE is an 80-minute dramatic presentation of God's epic story of redemption as revealed in the Bible. The HOPE uses existing Hollywood films with some original footage to create the framework whereby a ministry can "personalize" the video using storytellers from the specific target audience by shooting in front of a green screen..

The producer, Mars-Hill Production in Texas, charges a royalty and license fee. At the time of writing it was $2500 for larger people groups and $1500 for PGs under a million. With each, the "partners" get 5,000 royalty free copies and are charged 10% of production costs for each DVD over 5,000.

Mars-Hills has a very stringent translation process in which one translates the script into, say Vietnamese, and then the English is deleted and someone else back-translates it from Vietnamese to English. The script is then sent to Texas and MH reviews it to ensure that the essence of the English script is communicated. The first HOPE we did took 3 months in this back and forth process while the last only took 40 days!

Thailand

The Central Thai HOPE was done in partnership with CBN Siam. They handled translation, shooting, editing and DVD mastering. Other than the length of time CBN required (six months) there were virtually no production problems.

The Isaan version was contracted out to the Christian Communication Institute in Chiang Mai. Unfortunately, the main video person was going on furlough and although they shot all the original footage in their green screen studio we had to take it back in-house for the editing and DVD masters.

Myanmar

Burmese was contracted out to Voice of Peace in Chiang Mai. The project was beyond them and we had to assist them in lighting and editing.

When we started WA we decided to use CCIs studio but essentially do it in-house.

Vietnamese

Vietnamese was contracted out to The Music Group in HCMC. It was probably the easiest and most professional job except for the fact that the editor had so many versions on his HD. I went in to solve some of the editing problems, spending 8 hours in the studio. As it was late it took until midnight to render and make the DVD, which was delivered to my hotel. When I viewed it I realized they had rendered the wrong version and had to go back to VN to get the corrected DVD.

Distribution

Central Thai, Isaan, WA and Burmese are all distributed by Nation Entertainment, Box 10, Chiang Mai 50000. Copies are made and distributed in-country by others.

Vietnamese is distributed in VN by The Music Group in HCMC and is in bookstores and distributed through the HC and official churches.

Lessons Learned/Discussion Thoughts

The choice of an outside contractor is an essential part of the process. In the case of VN, The Music Group was the only choice as I had contracted out two Billy Graham films the year before. Because they were associated with the official church they had connections in the government and we were able to get it approved by the Vietnamese censors.

Mars Hill Production requires an extensive approval process for both establishing who is the lead adaptation partner as well as how the process will get done. It should not be taken lightly as time and details are involved.

In addition, Mars-Hill requires the collection of royalties and a quarterly reporting process of copies distributed and any fruit from the specific production.

Written by Dan Henrich - info@comresources.org

VIDEO/FILM CASE 11:
RANSOM TURKISH FILM

Category: Drama
Location: Turkey

The project was designed to make a clear presentation of the Good News using both dramatic and verbal expressions. We wanted to make visual, but with clear content, something of the heart, the 'kernel' of the Gospel.

Storyline: (DIRECTOR)

The film explores the relationship between two former university friends. Memduh lives with his family in Istanbul. He hasn't seen his friend Osman for a couple of years. But one day Osman appears on his doorstep out of breath after being chased.

As the story unfolds, amid action and dramatic tension, we learn that Osman is being chased in a blood feud. He has tried to cover his

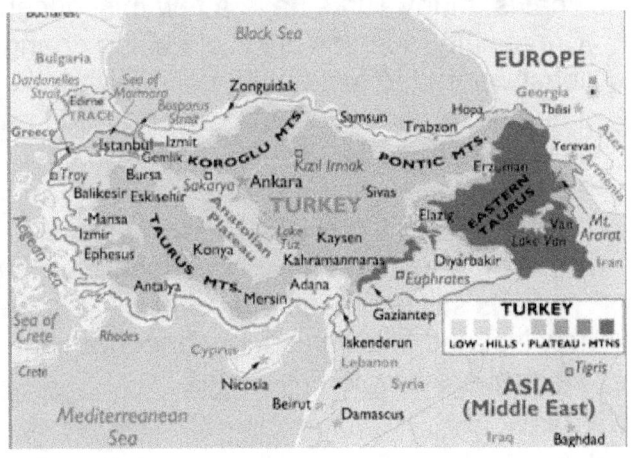

tracks and begin a new life. But the more he tries to keep the problem a secret, the more Memduh is dragged into the mess.

At the same time, Osman discovers that Memduh also has a secret that he is hiding: he has become a Christian. Various changes were made to the script for dramatic impact. It had mostly been written by people with very little film or TV experience. There was a point when the fact had to be addressed that there was far too much preaching in the content. There were many issues pertaining to the Muslim perceptions of Christianity which the sponsors wanted to address through the film. This demanded long dialogue sequences that the producer and I agreed could not all be included in one sixty-minute film. So some were cut, but there are still some verrrrry long dialogue scenes that only served to preach the message. (The best way to have approached the film would have been to spend extra time developing the script before entering into production.)

Strategic Objective

The production was very clearly meant to be 'evangelistic' in nature, with a few 'pre-evangelistic' "weed pullers" as well. That is, many Turks have a few misconceptions about Christianity, such as the Bible being changed, that we at least wanted to hint at in the film. When I started the project, I had never made a film before nor did I have any experience in such things.

I bought a book first of all, *How to Write a Script*. So, no, it wasn't meant to be a part of a longer term media effort. There is still not much of a 'church' to speak of in Turkey - a few isolated fellowships, but encouraging is the fact that several are now led by Turks.

Country/Region/Religion

Turkey (possibly with wider use in the Islamic world)

Language

Turkish (with possibilities to be dubbed...as it has been) into other Muslim languages.

Estimated audience

This is very difficult to say. In Turkish, we've sold more than 200 copies at Book Fairs in Turkey. So how many people see each one? Several hundred have been sold or distributed via Christian workers in Turkey. In Azerbaijan, it was aired late at night over State TV. How many saw it? It was also aired in the Middle East by CBN in Lebanon. How many actually saw it? ME TV reaches Lebanon, Israel, Syria, Jordon, Cyprus and part of Egypt.

Partnership Agency

Although we had tremendous support from Stuart Bennett at CBN, and Bob McLeod of Media Matters, nearly all of the money was raised by Spear Trust. It was a very low budget film, as is obvious. We had a partnership with Turgay, a keen, talented Turkish believer, who was the consultant on the script.
Script and production: Describe the script writing process. Was there research involved and by whom? As mentioned above, Turgay was the 'final word' on the Turkish content of the script; I had written it with 'a lot of help from my friends'. Bob McLeod and I think Stuart had to do some 'last minute' adjusting of scenes, dramatic aspects, etc. of the film while making it in Istanbul.

Research

I've spoken with ex-pats and Turkish believers, Azeri believers, and Kazak believers who all say, that for a first effort it is good; not great, but the purpose (a clear presentation of the Gospel with some dramatic aspects) was accomplished. The believers in Iran are still working to dub it...under less than friendly circumstances!

They believe it's worth it. Future: Do you plan to produce a follow-on production? What could have been done to improve the production or organizational relationship? We have produced a second film, *Ali and Silvana*, again with great help from Stuart Bennett and Bob McLeod. I raised almost all of the finances – again, a very low budget film.

DIRECTOR: Further pre-production would have greatly enhanced the project, and a couple of extra days of shooting would have increased the quality. More time was needed for casting (several of the minor roles were played by non-actors, which always shows on screen. More time would have translated into finding better actors.) Of course, a larger budget is always the cry of the director! But having said that, to accomplish what we did on location in Turkey with only a few Christians available to help, for $20,000, I think is truly amazing!

FMI: Roger Malstead rogerhm@attglobal.net

VIDEO/FILM CASE 12: CHILDREN'S FINGER PUPPET SERIES

Category: Drama
Location: Latin America

DEDITOS is a Bible story series targeting first the children of Guatemala, then Latin America and beyond. Based on the biblical passages, the programs are designed to reveal the character of God, the way he cares for each one of us and his never-ending desire that we draw closer to him.

Each story is told in roughly 23 minutes through real-life fingers, carefully crafted scenery and a dramatic sound track that breaths life and personality into the characters. The programs transport the viewer to biblical times, presenting God's provision for his children in the midst of dramatic conflicts.

Reasons for creating the project

Bible translation efforts have often put a priority on the New Testament. That focus has left many minority language groups without their own access to the stories of the Old Testament

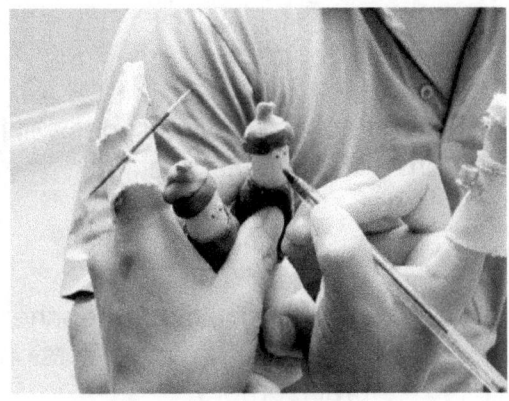

which provide the context for the New Testament.

Minority cultures by nature identify more with the practices and mindsets of people in the Old Testament stories. Each episode of *Deditos* provides them that opportunity and addresses the following:

> -The New Testament tells us that Jesus is the son of God. Without the background of when God created everything, it can be confusing in some cultures to draw the connection between the God of creation and Jesus, the only begotten son.

> - The *Deditos* stories also address the important theme of the existence of sin. Nearly all evangelistic efforts include some reference to turning from our individual sins, but without addressing the reign and dominion sin has over us. The stories of the Old Testament establish that powerful grip of sin and evil from which Christ makes us free.

> - Matthew's gospel begins with a detailed geneology of Jesus which often rings boring and irrelevant even to Christians. The stories of the Old Testament provide the important roots of these geneologies, revealing God's master plan for humanity.

Project description

The complete *Deditos* series will include 20 stories, mostly from the Old Testament.

Each episode includes:
- the story on a DVD
- a guide booklet for teachers with 5 Bible lessons
- a CD with an audio version of the guide booklet for oral learners

- individual pages of manual activities for children
- a song which can serve as a memory link with the story

Every story is lifted right from the pages of the Bible and crafted to utilize the impact which the medium of video can have.

Principals Guiding the Development of the Material

The videos are designed to facilitate translation into other languages.

The lessons are easy to translate and designed to be used by untrained teachers.

Each video captures the attention and heart of the viewer with the story. When used together with the lessons they:
- contribute to the unfolding story of God's great plan of redemption.
- reveal the unchanging character of God and his love for his people.
- develop themes respecting the intent of the biblical writers while also powerfully addressing realities lived today by children.
- place special attention on aspects of the Bible stories that challenge animistic practices. These points are further highlighted with specific applications in the lessons.

What these productions hope to achieve:
- give special attention to the population comprised of 4-to-14-year-olds in minority language groups in Latin America and elsewhere.
- tell the story of what God has done and how people have responded to the relationship he has offered us,

so as to better understand the human condition and the hope found only in Jesus Christ.
· motivate teachers and children to know and trust God by understanding the stories of the Bible and applying them to daily living.
· that people in minority language groups become aware of their own attitudes and change their behaviors based on new understanding of the plans God has for each person.

Why this medium?

Story is a powerful medium.
Story is a powerful format, producing a cause and effect reaction in both the mind and heart of a person. God's revelation in the Scriptures is primarily made through the medium of story.

In the context of minority language groups (the primary audience for this series), children grow up in a culture where oral tradition is the natural mechanism for transmitting values to the group. Stories, parables and proverbs become some of the key elements that hold their world view together, providing identity and a sense of belonging to the group.

NOTE: It has often been said, but it's worth reminding ourselves that for certain groups, receiving their information through the written word is not an option.

Forming thought patterns and values

The values and beliefs at the core of a child's world view are formed through stories at a very early age. It follows then that story is a highly effective way to redeem a culture and modify a world view to become Christ-centered.

A series of videos focused on God's story and his relationship to the world and humanity provides an important strategy for effecting real change in the lives of people.

The novel use of fingers promotes global acceptance and attracts audiences with wide diversities (such as personal preferences, criteria and stereo-types), because fingers look pretty much the same around the world regardless of race.

A series designed specifically for certain ethno-linguistic communities

This series has been designed with a special focus on ethno-linguistic groups who have an animistic perspective—people who believe themselves to live under the control of spirits and powers that rule over daily life. They live in a constant state of fear of the spirits, always seeking how to appease or manipulate them. *Deditos* demonstrates the power of God, contrasting it with the kingdom of Satan. It also teaches the relevance of the gospel for living a victorious life that is free from the fear of demonic forces.

Areas of usage

From the beginning *Deditos* was produced to be used among the Kakchiquels of Sololá, Guatemala. Teachers and missionaries from elsewhere in Guatemala and Latin America soon saw its potential for use with their own local groups. The first episode of the series has already been dubbed into the following languages:

- Chuj in Guatemala
- Poptí in Guatemala
- Ixil in Guatemala
- Kakchiquel in Guatemala
- Kekchí in Guatemala.
- Guaraní in Paraguay
- 3 languages in the Philippines

- Tzongo in Mozambique

Wide geographic and inter-confessional opportunities

From the beginning the determination was made to produce the stories deliberately avoiding contextualizing them for any one region or specific ethnic group. This strategy allows viewers to identify the stories as their own. The process of dubbing to other languages becomes much less complex and the translated materials are more readily accepted and assimilated by viewers (users).

The foundations for the scripts come straight from Scripture, avoiding particular confessional interpretations or specific denominational doctrines.

How is the series being produced?

The first four episodes have been produced by a multi-cultural team comprised of Mayans, Latins and North American missionaries.

The scripts were written by first extracting the stories from the pages of the Bible. Advanced dramatic scriptwriting techniques and language usage were then applied to best tell the Bible story through the chosen medium. The process also includes rigorous theological review.

To allow the fingers appearing as actors to express character and personality, the audio acting is recorded first. Once that process is completed the music is selected and the story first comes together in audio form.

The scenery is created using a variety of materials to create the textures and forms appropriate for the creative interpretations made regarding the biblical locations.

With the audio track as a guide (including the dialogue and music), the scenes are shot with the finger actors matching their movements to the sound track. The actors (fingers) perform on a three dimensional stage as depth of field is critical to this miniaturized production format. Every scene is carefully analyzed and the action is covered from multiple camera angles. Each shot is rehearsed and repeated until the team achieves a minimum of three good takes from at least three camera angles for each scene.

The abundance of useable takes then allows the editors to fulfill the vision of each scene. In post-production the video is carefully edited and visual effects (CG) are added to complement the shots, taking care to avoid competing with the childlike simplicity of the visual format of *Deditos*.

Some brief history

In Guatemala, as in much of Latin America, a large portion of the population is very young. 42.9% are 14 years of age or younger. Because of Viña's close relationship with churches in the rural sectors of the country and knowing how little attention is often given to these young boys and girls, they decided to design a production especially for them. The initial option considered was to dub animated films (cartoons), but when they sought permission from the international producers their request was turned down. So with almost no experience in video production, the idea of *Deditos* began to emerge.

In 2003 the creative and technical team at Asociación Viña produced the first episode. The Bible story chosen for this initial effort was "David and Goliath" in the Kaqchikel language. In those early efforts primary attention was given to the message they wanted to communicate. The creative element was important too along with the technical areas, but what they were able to achieve fell short of the standards required by the medium.

Approximately two years ago they began intentionally preparing producers, technicians and creative talent. The result of that ongoing training is now reflected in the presentation of the first package of programs.

Limitations

Although Viña continues to develop artists within their geographic location, there is still a shortage of people to act all of the characters the series will eventually require. In the technical areas they continually discover and develop innovative techniques to facilitate and enrich the production. The technical abilities of the staff are constantly developing, but with the endless details that emerge while working in miniature the time factor is always one of their biggest challenges.

Achievements in production

Episodes continue to be produced in less time. Creative sensibilities and improvement in quality control have advanced significantly for every member of the team.

Activities and strategies for usage, distribution and shared commitment

The strategic implementation plan for using *Deditos* is to involve:
1. National pre-primary and primary schools
2. Institutions dedicated to social programs for boys and girls
3. Churches (Sunday schools, vacation Bible schools and others)

4. NGO's and other international instituitions developing educational programs
5. Radio and television (both local transmission and cable)

Viña has initiated presentations of the videos and usage of the lessons in Kaqchikel churches in Sololá. With the help of a local indigenous promoter, they are inviting pastors and teachers to get involved. The whole program can be used by churches of different creeds as well as by diverse educational and social entities in the region.

Broadcasting

Deditos is a program that can be viewed at home, projected cinema-style or broadcast on television, cable or Internet. TV broadcasters in Guatemala have already expressed strong interest for including *Deditos* in their programming schedule.

Diverse kinds of licensing

Given their limited experience in the area of distribution, Viña is seeking and receiving advice about how to best approach this part of the process. *"Deditos has tremendous potential and we want to share it with ministries around the world".* José Abel de la Cruz, creator

Discussion

Although this project was developed for small media/DVD distribution among the smaller language groups of South/ Central Americas, could you see distribution for this in other areas of the world? If so, where and how. If not, why?

FMI: John Gowan johngowantv@gmail.com

VIDEO/FILM CASE 13: CAY CAU - THE BRIDGE

Category: Dramatic Film
Location: Vietnam

Cay Cau is the first Vietnamese language film to bring the message of the gospel in a culturally relevant format to the people of Vietnam. While other "Christian" films have been translated into Vietnamese, The Bridge *or* Cay Cau *was the first film based on an original Vietnamese screenplay.*

Synopsis

The film is about Dung and Phuong, a young man and woman living in present day Hanoi. Dung comes to faith in Christ through a mentoring relationship with Truong, a former gang leader who came to Christ while in prison. Dung takes care of his elderly infirm mother by selling fruit on the streets of Hanoi. Phuong is a pretty girl who lives a carefree life with her playboy boyfriend. Eventually, the true character of her boyfriend plays out and she finds herself as a jilted lover. True to Asian tragedy, Phuong suffers a debilitating accident and loses her eyesight. Phuong then lives a hand-to-

mouth existence selling fruit on the street. It is at this low point in her life that she meets Dung. While Dung has meager financial means to help her, he does have the greatest gift of all to share with her, the love of Jesus Christ. In order to make the best out of the dire circumstances that they both face, Phuong moves in with Dung to help nurse his dying mother. In the course of caring for the cantankerous old woman, Phuong models true love through serving her and in time leads her to Christ. The helpful catalyst for spreading the Good News from one person to the next is an old gospel tract telling the story of how Christ is the bridge over the chasm of sin and back into a relationship with the living God. The love of God and the old "Bridge" tract are shared from person to person throughout the story with the final recipient giving the tale a surprise twist ending.

Strategic Objectives

Every nation has a unique culture and history. Understanding the history of a country is paramount when creating media tools to be used for spreading the gospel. Vietnam has a history of Confucianism, ancestral worship, colonialism, Catholicism, imperialism, communism and capitalism. Addressing fundamental roadblocks leftover from the culture's checkered past required a story providing enough latitude to answer some of these old "roadblock" questions.

Northern Bias – Modern Vietnam became unified in 1975. The historic split between Communist North and Imperialist/ Colonialist South happened in 1954. The '54 watershed year saw thousands of Vietnamese Christians flee southward ahead of the Communist rule. This dash for freedom established the idea that Christians are more loyal to the south. Since the end of the Vietnam War most of the Christian evangelistic media has been produced using the southern dialect or word choices. These materials are less credible to Northern Vietnamese. The northern dialect is used to broadcast the national news, translate foreign films and is spoken by all those who stayed behind in the north and ultimately won the war. This is why *The Bridge* is a Hanoi-based story using only native Hanoi speakers.

Basic Misconceptions – After years of being spoon-fed propaganda, the general public has a plethora of misconceptions about what it means to be a "Christian". Some of these ideas that are challenged in the course of telling this story are: Christians are not true patriots, Christianity is from Europe and has no place in Asia, Christians don't respect the memory of their ancestors. While combating these ideals was not the main purpose for creating the film, it was deemed important to address these gross misconceptions during the telling of the story. It is hoped that the story will shed new light on what it truly means to be "Christian."

Metaphors not Doctrine – When addressing the teaching moments in the film, it is accomplished via example, not by simply stating, "The Bible says". In one scene a rose is on the dinner table and is used to tell of how God's love is diffused through His children like fragrance comes from a flower. The film was created more to model Christian living than to instruct on Christian conduct.

Affinity Groups – The setting of the capital city of Hanoi, Vietnam provides a strategic location for other Southeast Asian people groups. Culturally, Vietnam is very similar to China and other Buddhist countries such as Cambodia, Thailand and Laos. Just by locale, Hanoi makes for a much more relational location for other Southeast Asian peoples than say Youngstown, Yuma or Spokane. By producing a story based in Southeast Asia the potential for reaching other neighboring cultures and countries is vastly enhanced.

Status: *The Bridge* has been translated from the original Vietnamese into English, Tagalog and Cantonese. Additional translations are underway for Thai and Mandarin. The film was originally released in Vietnam in 2006-07 and subsequently released in the USA in 2008. The Philippine release was 2008 and the China release 2009. A Thai subtitled release was distributed in 2008. All current language translations are available for viewing on *vimeo* or by going to www.greatpearlmissions.org The producers are open to any person or organization that may want to champion the translation of the film into other languages.

Areas of Use

The original film was distributed throughout much of the northern and central regions of Vietnam through local churches. Fifty thousand copies of the film were given away through this church network. Copies of the film have now reached most of the country through organic "friend to friend" distribution. Over 4000 copies of the film have been sold in the USA with multiple language capability. All of the main Vietnamese population centers in the USA have been supplied with the film including Los Angeles, San Diego, San Jose, Houston, Dallas, Atlanta and Chicago. *The Bridge* was television broadcast in "Little Saigon," Westminster, California over the local Vietnamese language station in 2010. Additional Master Copies of the film were provided for strategic distribution purposes to Australia, Moscow and Paris, which are major expat Vietnamese population centers. Public showings of the film were conducted through church outreaches across Malaysia for Vietnamese guest workers residing there.

Estimated Audience

Vietnam and China are considered closed countries for evangelistic activities. The numbers provided for Vietnam and USA distribution are accurate. However translating these distribution numbers into estimated audience numbers is purely speculative. Potential viewing audience base only on language capability: Vietnamese 89 million, Cantonese 70 million, Tagalog 65 million, English 500 million to 1.8 billion.

Production

The Bridge was produced by Greatpearl Missions of Richland, Michigan and Gospel Communications International (GCI) of Muskegon, Michigan. After production of *The Bridge*, GCI has since closed its doors, but Greatpearl Missions continues operations. Producers of the film were husband-and-wife team Scott and Lien Sweezie. Executive Producers were Mr. Billy Zeoli, Mr. Robert Sweezie and Mr. J.R. Whitby. Production and distribution costs in their entirety were approximately $500, 000 USD. These funds were raised over the course of the four-year project.

Script and Production

The Bridge film was based on a story written by Mr. Scott Sweezie. The screenplay was written by a Hanoian who wrote the dialogue using colloquial phraseology. By having the original screenplay written in Vietnamese first and not English, it allowed for a more fluid natural dialogue. Additionally, the film offers true-to-life colloquial idioms, making the story all the more real to people living in Hanoi. An English-to-Vietnamese translation would have been choppy and off the mark in terms of local patterns of speech.

The film was shot on location in Nong Kai, Thailand and Hanoi, Vietnam. Mr. Heinz Fussle of GCI was director. Heinz's guidance during the course of the whole film making process was instrumental in making this film become a reality. Freedom Films of Chang Mai, Thailand provided all of the Thai production work under the guidance of Mr. Tom Silkwood. Freedom Films also provided postproduction services from their Chang Mai television studio. All of the dialogue scenes and action sequences were filmed in Nong Kai because it has a large indigenous Vietnamese-Thai population from which to draw cast. It was by necessity that the film was made outside of Vietnam due to the nature of the content. The B-roll footage was shot on location in Hanoi, Vietnam. The Hanoi footage provides views of well-known Vietnamese landmarks and lends the film authenticity.

The original music score was written and performed by Mr. Gene Ort of Gene Michael Productions of South Bend, Indiana. The world-renowned dan bau performer Mr. Pham Duc Thanh granted additional performances on the Vietnamese dan bau instrument. The dan bau gives a hauntingly beautiful sound indigenous only to Vietnam.

Research and Character Development

The Bridge's producers Scott and Lien Sweezie moved to Hanoi in 2001. Lien is a Vietnamese-American who had originally come to the US after the fall of Saigon in 1975. Moving to Hanoi offered the couple a unique opportunity to view ordinary life in modern day Vietnam and to assimilate what they experienced there with their faith in God. The desire to see all people come to know Jesus for themselves led them to create this film. Learning of the real life hardships that many Vietnamese endure gave them key insights into how to craft a believable story. Above all, the story itself needed to be believable. Locations, names, and activities had to ring true. If the story grew to be too "Hollywood" it would take away from the underlying message of God's love being shared from one person to another.

Inspiration for two of the characters in the film is actually derived from one man in real life, Mr. Tinh of Hai Phong. In the film the mentor to the hero was in times past a gangster, but had turned from his old ways after he became a new creation in Christ. The film's leading lady Phuong becomes blind through an accident, but it's only after she loses her eyesight that she see's Jesus for the first time. Mr. Tinh was a gangster in the port city of Hai Phong. He was big, handsome and a force to be reckoned with. One day a rival gang threw a jar of acid in his face as he drove his motor scooter down the street. Tinh became blind, disfigured and helpless. He attempted suicide on several occasions. Everyday he would wake up, go downstairs, pull his chair up to the wall and start to pound his head against it begging to die. One day a man came to him and told him about Jesus. He now has a reason for living. He is not afraid to tell anyone and everyone about Jesus. Today he embraces life rather than begging for it to end. Mr. Tinh is a very successful businessman and has a wonderful family with two children. It is his life that helped to breathe life into these two characters in *The Bridge*. He still is blind, but now he sees.

Discussion Questions

How do you see these real life stories fitting into the evangelism process? Can you think of stories where you work that are like this? Video/Film Case 9 is very similar as it was taken from a real story told by a field worker.

Start collecting these types of stories for possible production in your area.

FMI: Scott Sweezie - ssweezie@gmail.com

Section Two:
Radio and Audio

Radio/Audio Case 1: FM Radio

Category: FM Radio
Location: Cambodia - Khmer

More than 12,000 Khmer children send responses to the 15-minute Chronological Bible Stories that are aired on twelve FM radio stations in Cambodia. Children draw what they remember about the stories that they learn on radio and send them to TWR through volunteers in the local churches, as the postal system in Cambodia functions poorly. The Lord brings hope in a dysfunctional oral society to use media creatively to influence the minds and hearts of the little ones!

Strategic Objective

The broad sowing media activity propels strong networking and coordination at the ground level as TWR learned to network with over 500 churches, from which 51 Khmer believers help coordinate 51 children's clubs in churches where kids from neighborhoods gather once every week to listen to the Bible stories. In 2008, a total of more than 300 kids professed their

faith in Christ at these children clubs.

Broad sowing of God's Word will never return in vain. A woman in Cambodia who had traded her child was listening to the TWR *Women of Hope* radio program, which was talking on the issue of trafficking, and the Spirit of God convicted this woman. She bought her child back from trafficking. What lessons do we learn from these experiences to use media strategically to reach oral communities?

The lessons learned in using mass media to reach children, women and youth of the unreached Khmer people group became the learning ground to prayerfully venture to reach the majority of the Khmer unreached people group with the truth of the Gospel. As Samnang, a trained Bible college pastor, attended orality training he knew how valuable it would be to use oral learning methods to reach the Khmer oral society. The Lord slowly unfolded each steps in the process enabling Samnang to develop a media strategy.

Area of Its Use

The unreached Khmer of Cambodia - primarily an oral society

Estimated Audience

Khmer people are the predominant ethnic group in Cambodia, accounting for approximately 90% of the 14.8 million people in the country. Because it is aired on twelve FM stations, it has a significant reach. Audience is unknown.

How was it produced?

Samnang and a team of five people conducted worldview studies and media habit studies among 100 Khmer people living in 20 different villages in Cambodia. Samnang says that in an oral community the researcher is seen as a stranger, as people wonder why they are sought to answer questions. He goes on further to say that people are willing to answer questions other than religious worldview questions, but the moment you start asking faith related questions they suspect the researcher must be from a Christian group and then it becomes a challenge to get answers. The lesson learned was to gather worldview information after establishing relationships over a period of time as relationship-building is essential in oral communities to share information.

Having done the worldview and media usage habit studies, Samnang and his team leader Veasna decided to meet with Pastor Barnabas who is known for his story telling to the Buddhist world. Having accepted the Lord from a Khmer Buddhist monk family background, Pastor Barnabas is one who understands the Khmer people's worldview and with his spiritual gifting tells Bible stories in many villages in Cambodia. As Samnang and Veasna wanted to partner with Pastor Barnabas in using media to tell stories, they heeded the advice of Pastor Barnabas to focus on a prayer strategy before launching the intended project.

In developing broad sowing strategy, Samnang used the worldview to create a list of story sets building bridges to the Khmer worldview. Pastor Barnabas the Regional Director for Ambassador for Christ came forward to record the stories, thus enabling quality story telling and recording in the Khmer language.

To reinforce the message, each story is composed into songs according to the traditional musical genre. The Lord enabled Samnang to identify Khmer believers who are gifted in writing poetry, composing poetry into lyrics and music, and singing in their traditional Khmer format. Another lesson learned is that these songs become major resources to the local church to use in their effort to reach the unreached, and also become a bridge to communicate God as not only the God of Jacob, but also the God of the Khmer people.

Samnang field tested the 30-minute radio programs which were done using oral learner's principles of dialog, story, and song format to present the truths of the Gospel. Field testing was done with 35 oral communicators gathered from 24 villages. Lessons learned were that the oral communicators preferred stories longer than 30 minutes which included many songs. Unfortunately cost factors confine the radio program to 30 minutes!

Based on the media usage habit study Samnang selected four FM radio stations that would cover five major provinces (Siem Reap, Banthey Meanchey, Battambang, Kandal and Kampong Speu) and Phnom Penh City as well. Due to limitations in funding the broadcasting will be done once a week. To build an effective reach, three days of broadcasting is preferred to help the oral audience to remember and recollect the stories.

Lessons Learned/Discussion Points

Many lessons have been learned in the process. The research activity that began in August 2007 along with prayer networking, partnerships, story and song development, and fundraising have taken a time frame of two years before the broadcasting of stories began in September 2009. The lessons learned were to trust in the Lord for Him to open doors and pour out His resources, to work in unity among the Khmer believers and expat missionaries.

What impact can we make when community development ministries collaborate with media ministries to create public education information such as farming, health, family education, moral values, and poverty elevation using oral learner principles? If Christian media ministries can broadcast these messages it can create a greater reach and awareness and impact. Focused media such as solar powered audio devices can also be distributed for group or community learning.

Complementing public education information, Bible stories can impart scriptural worldview in the society, bringing them to the knowledge of the almighty God and of the Savior.

Closer collaboration between media ministries and other field-related missions can complement the Kingdom's work strategically. If we consistently broadcast seven days a week it will help in building an audience to whom we can minister through different ministries in their respective local areas.

Further collaboration with local churches can be enhanced if church buildings will be used for community related work during week days thus opening doors for stronger collaboration between para-church organizations and the local churches to collectively meet the needs of the oral society. Focused media can be provided as a bridge to the oral society to learn and grow.

FMI : Andrew Sundar - <u>asundar@twr.org</u>

Radio/Audio Case 2: Never Too Late Radio

Category: Radio
Location: Thailand

In an effort to reach middle class Thais, a 120-episode radio drama was co-written by an experienced Thai writer in partnership with expat media experts.

This project involves a strategy to place dramatic radio programs on primarily AM band radio. We have identified the dramatic radio production company KATHIP in Bangkok. KATHIP is the longest running dramatic radio producer in Thailand. Currently they have nine series on the air with 50-60 thirty-minute episodes each. Most of them are love triangle, action adventure series. Some are just radio re-writes of soaps or stories in magazines.

KATHIP is a full service company – they write and produce the dramas, get advertiser support and buy radio time. They also do fulfillment, for example, if a tee shirt is offered by those who write

in, KATHIP packages and mails it out. The targets of most of KATHIP's dramas are not in cities and are a lower class demographic such as a vegetable- or flower-seller. Some of KATHIP's dramas are on FM radio and are by nature different. We plan to have a joint venture with KATHIP where a Thai Christian creative team develops the characters, storylines and scripts. KATHIP produces and markets the series. We have a website and follow up mechanism, feeding respondents to those on the ground.

Objective

The goal will be to create characters who have:
• Credibility—Is the character believable as the bearer of the message?
• Attractiveness—Is the character attractive or appealing?
• Similarity—Does the character have anything in common with the listeners?
• Authority and expertise—Does the character likeable enough to lead the listeners to consider other behavior?

Strategy

In an attempt to understand the broad strategy developed for this project, one must understand the communication theory underpinnings:
Social Learning Theory is concerned with how individual people make sense of the social environment and decide what to do.People learn by:
• Observing what other people do;
• Considering the consequences experienced by those people;
• Rehearsing what might happen in their own lives if they followed the other people's behavior;
• Taking action by trying the behavior themselves;

• Comparing their experiences with what happened to the other people;
• Confirming their belief in the new behavior.
• Modeling takes place when people observe others performing a behavior either in real life or in a drama.
• Find them attractive or admirable;
• Feel they have something in common with them, and have an emotional reaction to them (usually inspired by the models' expressions of emotion).
• Efficacy describes a feeling of personal empowerment, of confidence in one's ability to perform a particular deed. Drama constantly employs vicarious efficacy. As listeners become emotionally involved with a character, for example, a shy young girl named Rose, her actions and personality inspire the listeners with the belief that "if Rose can do it, so can I."

Methodology

A working group was gathered for several days to:

1. Develop character descriptions
The goal will be to create characters who have:
• Credibility—Is the character believable as the bearer of the message?
• Attractiveness—Is the character attractive or appealing?
• Similarity—Does the character have anything in common with the listeners?
• Authority and expertise—Does the character likeable enough to lead the listeners to consider other behavior?
Change: how does the character change over the series? For example, does he/she gamble more or less? Curse more or less?
Usually there are two opposing characters, one whose life gets worse when he/she continues doing the negative behavior, the other whose life changes when they change.

2. Develop script outlines for 30 episodes.

3. Write five scripts in the series. This should be at very least the story written in short story format, as opposed to full dialogue.

4. Plan out successive series
For example: Series One will introduce all the characters.
Eps 1-10: The situation with the gambling is stressed. Borrowing of the dowry. Debt.
Eps 11-20: Boy meets girl. Discussions with his peers on wanting sex. AIDs brought up. Boy tries to seduce girl on dare. Accident. Hospital. Boy is despondent. Father meets boy.
Eps 21-30: Father tells his history of drinking, womanizing and how he met an older man who told him his story and how the younger Father wanted to be like him.

Outcomes

From this initial grouping, 30 episodes were written and produced by KATHIP. The episodes were aired on a Bangkok FM station and Kathip found the series so likable that they they put it on the Thai Government AM station!

Funding was located and eventually 120 episodes were produced that chronicled the lives of Annop, the father, Chaba, the mother, Noon the handicapped girl, her boyfriend, and a host of other characters that included an AIDS victim, gamblers and a gangster! Christine Henrich completed her MA Thesis in an analysis of the letters and SMS messages. A White Paper is available at http://www.comresources.org/?page_id=9. See Radio/Audio Case 3 for detailed character descriptions.

Written by Dan Henrich - info@comresources.org

Radio/Audio Case 3: Never Too Late Radio

Category: Radio
Location: China

Following the success of the Thai NTL radio series (see Radio/Audio Case 2), a partnership was established with a national media company for the adaption of the storylines into Chinese and marketing of the series to China National Radio....

Strategy

Using the English back-translations as a basic storyline the national partner agreed to (in the original MOU):

1.   Translate and localize the existing episodes to best communicate the basic entertainment-education episodes to communicate the messages in an effective manner within the Chinese culture.

2.   Research the methods by which dramatic radio programs are produced and aired on China National Radio (CNR) and determine the most economical and most effective way to air the

programs to reach the largest audience.

3.   Upon approval of the back translation of the initial ten test episodes, they will be produced and presented to CNR for approval. In the event that CNR approves the episodes for production, the partner will produce up to 50 episodes, negotiate airtime with CNR and coordinate follow-up of the responses

Status

After the production of what turned out to be 35 fifteen-minute contracts the partner decided that they did not have the time or the interest to fulfill the contract and do the marketing and placement. This was a setback to the project as we had put our trust in this partner and they just decided that they were not interested.

So, after several emails back and forth, I took a copy of the highlighted MOU and showed it to him. This person took a number of evasive verbal turns. My goal was to maintain the relationship but the partner had bigger fish to fry and was not interested in continuing.

Disposition

We created a website, http://www.weishibuwan.com/ (*Never Too Late* in Chinese) which streams the radio programs in Mandarin with English script. The programming is available for free. It has been streamed many times on the Hipcast podcast and we have promoted it on offshore Chinese radio sites.

Storyline (common for NTL Thai - Radio/Audio Case 2 and NTL China)

NEVER TO LATE is a 120-episode radio drama about a family.

Here are the Character sketches:

The husband and father **Anop** is a good and honest man (50 years old) who loves his wife and one daughter and a niece who is like a daughter to him and works long hours each week to try to meet the family's growing financial needs. He is closer to the daughter, and he sees her as being more innocent and needing more watching over. He is away too much but when he is at home he takes time to show his wife and daughter that he really loves them. He is optimistic and hopeful for the future of both his daughters.

Chaba (45 years), the wife and mother, should be happy with her life and family, but she is not. This is mostly due to the fact that she has never gotten over the reality that she married a much less wealthy man. Her family before had provided her with every luxury, including someone to cook and clean for her. But her family lost their wealth when she was a young woman through a series of bad investments. So she ended up settling for Anop, then a manager employee of her father. She loves and respects him now, but still longs for more. Though she and Anop have been married several years and she now has Pawr, the niece who is like a daughter, and Noon, their real daughter, Chaba just cannot be happy with her situation. She is closer to her niece even though very disappointed that Pawr did not score well enough and they could not afford college for her. It still bothers Chaba that Pawr was only able to find a job at a local factory. She constantly tries to spend time with her old female school friends, who mostly married well or inherited fortunes and have money to spare. When she is with them it helps her forget her current level of financial ability and status. Of course, most of the time they play mahjong and gamble, which she cannot afford to do. So her darkest secret from her husband and the girls right now is her huge and growing gambling debt.

Pawr - The oldest niece, Pawr, only finished one year of college and now works at a factory. She has secretly been dating a guy at work and has recently fallen in love with him. They have already been sexually active for some weeks. His name is San and he comes from an even poorer family than hers. He is a hard worker and is definitely in love with Pawr, but he knows there will be problems ahead in their relationship. The biggest and next problem is that he wants to get married soon. He drives a very old scooter back and forth to work from the slum part of town. And that is just one sign that he has no money for the dowry or to properly support Pawr. So far Pawr has been unwilling to even introduce him to her family.

Noon (21 years), the real daughter, is a very innocent but pretty young lady in her third year of college. She is smart and has a scholarship from her father's company. She is popular enough with kids from her status and social level, so she has plenty of friends. But, she has never really had a boyfriend or that "first love." That's about to change and so is every other part of her life.

Pagpoom (22 years) is also a student at the university but comes from a very wealthy family. His father is totally out of the picture and he hardly ever sees his socialite and executive mother. He is a playboy with all the toys, including a snazzy new car. Pagpoom is always looking for his next girlfriend and there are plenty chasing after him. He runs with the loud and proud young rich boys and girls at the university and spends more time partying nights than doing well in his studies. After all, he knows he will inherit the company and the family fortune someday. His life is also about to make a drastic change

Written by Dan Henrich - info@comresources.org

Radio/Audio Case 4:
Dramatic Radio
Philippines

Category: Dramatic Radio
Location: Manila, Philippines

In order to continue to sow the Gospel broadly the Philippines Baptist Mission Mass Media (PBM-MM) began to explore what genres of radio programming were most popular and how could MM move into these channels of communication.

The Baptist Hour Choir had already been showing on TV on Sunday afternoon and heard three or four different times per week on several of the most popular AM radio stations. In the beginning this was about 10 stations located in the 10 largest cities of the Philippines. It is not an exaggeration to say that a well-placed program would be able to be heard virtually throughout the Philippines. It was already obvious that rather than watching TV, Filipinos listened to the radio all day long and into the evenings, and of course, a large majority of Filipino households and businesses had radios. This was evident when going into a more rural village. The sport of boxing was a favorite and during the showing of a TV boxing program one could observe 30 to 50 people of all ages, squeezing together outside the one house that had TV to get a peek and hear the boxing match.

However, anyone and everyone and most businesses had radios blaring all day long.

The most popular radio programs in the urban setting included music radio programming, "magazine-style" talk shows with a male and female host, and the "Filipino radio drama – soap opera."

The Baptist Hour Choir was already enjoying a good listenership during music radio programming, often without having to pay for airtime. So, MM-PBM began to research the early morning talk show and the soap opera – ongoing dramatic radio programming. It was decided to begin with just the radio drama program.

After some experimentation in the Tagalog radio audience in Manila and Cebuano audience in Cebu (the two largest cities and most powerful radio stations), the radio drama series began to be fleshed out into what topics and how long the run of each topic and how they could/should overlap over time.

Over several months the direction for the radio drama and main cast of characters and subject matter/story line became clear. The program would focus on social problems common to many Filipinos and households: alcoholism, gambling, spouse abuse, financial problems, emotional-stress problems, loneliness, spiritual problems and questions, etc. The program topics and actual scripts would be developed, written and tested as a team by what is now known now as the International Baptist Mission (IMB) personnel and PMB staff. There was a specific decision to not allow the program to become too "religious" or "preachy" in its content or image.

Radio voice talents would be enlisted and directed to do the actual drama recordings in the local radio station studios. Utilizing existing professional voice talents accomplished two important things. One, these talents were well known as they did several of the different soap opera radio programs on several stations. They were celebrities who had a "followership" of listeners. Two, using the secular existing radio talents helped insure that the program would sound like a normal radio program on the air. At first, the announcer was also a professional radio talent and did the lead in and close out invitation to respond. Eventually MM decided to utilize a Christian counselor, who also happened to be well known for being a part of the Baptist Hour Choir and doing commercials.

Early on, as these programs were written, rehearsed and aired, an important idea surfaced among the FMB directors and the PBM staff. These talents and the radio producers and technicians needed to be the focus of specific and ongoing witnessing by anyone and everyone who had contact with them from MM-PBM. God really blessed this idea and the commitment of the staff to pray for these people by name.

The nuclear family would be a typical extended family in one dwelling place including grandparents, their married son and his wife, young daughters, sons. Other significant personalities would be extended family, such as aunt and uncle, neighbors and workplace persons like boss, and co-workers.

The response would be by mail (still not many phones in households and expensive, so not the usual way people responded to radio). A strategy for the follow-up materials was developed to highlight response to the particular dramatic "focus problem" from each week's drama. These were aired five days a week, very early morning and late afternoon, and some also in late evening. The announcer who gave a quick synopsis of the last few days and opened the "scene" of the day's program also ended with the invitation to respond. As with most drama programs, Friday always ended with some "cliff hanger" and the announcer usually asked some dramatic question of the listeners. "Will Joseph really steal his grandmother's broach and sell it to buy more drugs?" Each day's program was clearly labeled by a number and the date aired.

They also spent a good deal of time discussing "topics" or "directions" of the drama. One important question was asked regularly: Are people opening up to hear God's truth or the Gospel as as a result of the program and our responses back to them?

Within the second year or so, it became apparent that someone with counseling experience who also knew the Filipino language and culture was needed to help train and direct the PMB staff to do the response. A couple with more than four years of experience on the field and a background in pastoral counseling was enlisted. During this process it became obvious that several of these basic themes/problems were going to cycle through the drama.

So specific tracts with Bible verses and encouragement and advice were developed. The gathering of the basic data on the responders and the process of re-connecting the responder to the same PMB staff counselor was also an important process and task.

The Bible Correspondence Course ministry - Mabuting Balita sa Inyo! (Good News to You) At some point midway through the second full season it was decided to move from just tracts on topics with verses to sending a 3-4 page piece on the topics along with an invitation to join a Bible study correspondence course. After the decision was made, MM-PBM looked at existing EV and church planting materials already available in the language. There was a series of five tract pieces developed by Charlie Brock for church planting – *Mabuting Balita sa Inyo!* - moving the student from Why study the Bible? How to do so? How to pray? and on to other discipleship topics: "Now you are a Christian – What's Next? Why have a daily devotion and how to do one, etc. - to joining a local church and eventually one on starting your own house church was added.

MM-PBM decided to adapt this series and use it as the core first course. Looking at several different BCC courses in the states and what other GCC groups were doing with BCC courses in the Philippines, the PBM team began the process of adapting the "Good News to You" series. They also developed the database system for gathering and organizing the students and their progress, and the contact responder and which missionary or local church was closest to them with other fields on dates, location, topics or situations discussed. (This was all in WordStar and sadly that is the reason we have none of the database anymore. Between two moves of the mission office and the mass media ministry and Wordpress replacing WordStar being replaced by MS Word – there were no survivors).

Through the next years of the radio program's life and the expansion to a BCC of 10,000 plus active students, the materials were refined to adjust to the kinds of questions students had and suggestions from pastors and church planter missionaries. MM-PBM "field tested" a lot of the materials by giving them to church planters and asking them to use them in their Bible studies as they did evangelism, discipleship and church planting. This yielded a lot of useful information on what worked and what didn't. Most notable was simply the need for less new information per lesson and more encouragement and review.

Keep in mind that these BCC materials were printed and going out and coming back through the Philippine mail system. The 3 - 4 page materials on topics were converted into lessons: Assurance: How to know you are a Christian. Authority of the Bible: Why study the Bible? How to study the Bible. Discipleship: How to have a meaningful relationship with God. Several were on topics like: Finding personal peace. Dealing with loss – grief. What is a Christian (biblical) response to abuse? How to share the Gospel. How to lead a Bible study, and others.

Conclusion

The Bible Correspondence program was turned over to the local church in an effort to reduce cost and this sounded the death knell. Within a short period of time the BCC closed up and expatriate personnel transferred elsewhere. The masters of the radio program were lost as the Mass Media department building was sold and the majority of these tapes lost.

Discussion Questions

If someone approached you today to help them develop a series of dramatic radio programs what would be your first step? You have been based in this country for some years. Have you developed a network of GCC media folk who might partner in the production phase?

How would you take the next step to develop a plan for research? Have you ever conducted a focus group? (See Appendix 1 - A Simple Guide to Media Research).

Edited by Dan Henrich - info@comresources.org

Radio/Audio Case 5: "Thoughts for Life"

Radio Thailand

Category: FM Radio
Location: North Thailand

"Thoughts for Life" radio program targets non-Christian listeners with popular music and practical advice based on Biblical principles.

Strategic Objective

To change preconceived ideas about Christianity so that listeners will be willing to hear the Gospel. Target audience is Northern Thai non-Christians age 30-50. Most Northern Thais, 98%, claim Buddhism as their religion. Christianity has been in Northern Thailand for 150 years, but less than 0.7% of the Northern Thai People are Christian. The program was designed to be a tool to be used by local churches and Christian groups to play on a community radio station in their area. Listeners can contact the producer and the sponsor church by post, email, phone, or SMS. Face to face contact and personal witness is the ultimate objective.

Area of its Use

The program has been used in select Northern Thai communities since mid 2009.

Phrae municipality. Three radio stations reach a population area of 100,000 Mon.-Sat. each with a one hour time slot. Two are commercial community radio stations. Time is purchased by a local church and a Christian mission organization. The third is a church operated community radio station.

Chiang Mai, SanSai area (population and radio audience unknown). Church operated community radio station M-F one hour time slot. Church does own follow up. No data.

Chiang Rai, Wiang Papao district (population 65,000 but radio audience unknown). Christian radio station, but not church operated. Sat. and Sun., one hour time slot.

Estimated Audience

Program is designed to be used by local churches in targeted areas by broadcast on small community radio stations. Centralized contact info is included in each program and is managed by the program producer, Mr. Bandhit Darwin. Listeners can contact by post, email, phone, or SMS. Mr. Bandhit fields 20 to 30 contacts per month, most contacts are made by phone and SMS. Mr. Bandhit follows up with Christian materials and media, captures their contact info in a database, and tries to arrange a personal meeting. In addition, a custom spot can be inserted into each program going to a specific community allowing listeners to directly contact the sponsor church in their area. We do not have feedback data from individual churches.

How was it produced?

The "Thoughts for Life" radio program's production, distribution, and followup is supported by an IMB project called Northern Thai Ministry under the supervision of

IMB missionary, Mark Patenaude. Mr. Bandhit earned a degree in theology and a masters degree in communication and is a licensed radio broadcaster. Mr. Bandhit records the hour long program at his home recording studio and distributes a week's worth of programs on CD to participating stations by mail. Recently, a Thai Christian organization supported by Thai Christian businessmen donated web space to host *Thoughts for Life* on the Internet (http://www.whitedream.thaifm.net/podcast/?p=home). Consequently, distribution has expanded to several new radio stations across the country.

Current status? Where aired?

Currently in the third year of broadcasting in the Phrae area and are in the follow up stage. We are able to enter villages and meet listeners face to face in homes. In March, a volunteer team from the Thailand Baptist Seminary in Bangkok came to follow up and do a listener survey. The team met many listeners that did not contact the feedback loop, but are regular listeners to program.

102 listener surveys were completed. The residents were receptive to the volunteers because they were associated with radio program. Listeners said they like the lessons in the program. Listeners tend to prefer live broadcasting over pre-recorded programs, but they still like to listen because the message is useful and helpful.

The messages center around family, relationships and marriage, and give words of encouragement to be excellent in all they do. The program seems to be a good entry activity that allows Christian teams to enter new communities with credibility and a good perception, facilitating relationship building and Christian witness.

FMI: Mark P - thaiteam@mac.com

98

Radio/Audio Case 6:
Local Radio Station

Category: FM Radio
Location: Chiang Mai, Thailand

The Government of Thailand opened the door to establish "low power" FM stations in the late 1990s and Thai businessmen snapped them up. Most had no experience in running the stations and soon realized they were more of a drain than a support to their business.

FM 104 came on the market in Chiang Mai in 2004 and a Thai pastor developed a partnership with a Christian printing company and several individual Christian missionaries to purchase the station for about $10,000. The station was run at the same location and we started discussions on how to brand the station and get advertising to support it. Eventually it was called CityLink FM.

Strategy

In 2006-7 more frequencies were opened up and a couple of Christian organizations snapped up the frequencies and started running preaching and teaching

messages and overt traditional Christian music. A couple of Thai churches used their stations as a "megaphone" and sermons were heard!

Campus Crusade Canada found a donor to partially fund 100 stations and we were asked by a GCC partner to meet with a committee in Bangkok to discuss programming for these stations as we had produced *Never Too Late*, a popular pre-evangelistic series that had reached many Thais.

I proposed the production of a series of pre-evangelistic programs much like *Never Too Late* and the other two series. The donors, three Christian businessmen from from Canada, were convinced that they only needed to get the stations on the air and the local committees would take care of programming. The plan was that three local Thai churches would partner together and raise 50% of the necessary capital (about $15,000). CCC would train a Disc Jockey(DJ) from each church with management and DJ skills. In addition, CCC was starting a repository of Christian music and teaching that these new stations could utilize. No attempt was made to encourage the stations to run secular music or felt-need talk shows to attract an audience.

CityLink-Chiang Mai

In 2009, CityLink's original location was lost to the station. On top of these problems, CityLink-Chiang Mai started to have transmitter problems. The station had inherited an old Thai manufactured unit that was overheating. HCJB-Global, a radio ministry founded in 1931 as a Christian shortwave station came to the rescue and donated a high quality 600-watt transmitter manufactured by Crown Broadcasting. This unit was installed by HCJB engineer, John Brewer. Several months later, that new transmitter failed and Brewer installed a new unit.

FM 104 CityLink worked with us to re-tool the *Never Too Late* (NTL) dramatic radio series for distribution in a programming block with music and to other low power and program hungry stations. The 120 episodes of NTL aired on stations in 36 provinces in Thailand several years ago. (See Radio/Audio Case 2 - Dramatic Radio Thailand)

Status

In late 2010 CityLink lost its 2nd location because the rent was raised and the station sits in a box. It is in need of a new antenna also.

The original Thai pastor has moved to Bangkok and the station needs additional capital. The plan is to move it to the Christian printing company as soon as funds are raised for the new antenna.

Conclusion

It seems clear that just replicating the format of Christian stations in the USA will not reach the majority of the Thai Buddhist population. Though there are disagreements on the number of evangelical believers in Thailand it is generally agreed that is is under one percent of the 67 million population.

Discussion Questions

What approach would you take to advise them on programming style and content?

How would you find out what the felt needs are in Thailand?

How would you develop linkages with radio trainers to help CityLink's management create these programs that would reach the lost?

FMI: Dan Henrich - info@comresources.org

Radio/Audio Case 7:

Ankan Indian Radio Outreach

Category: FM "Jungle" Radio
Location: Jungles of Suriname

Our Strategic Objective is to get the Gospel to the remote tribal groups in the Jungles of Suriname, South America.

Area of Use (target group): Our target group is the Aukan people, but we are also reaching the Paramaccan, Aluku, Saramaccan, Trio, Wyana, and Matawai tribes as well.

Estimated Audience Our target Audience is about 10,000 Aukaners but we have probably another 20,000 other tribal listeners.

How was it produced? Terry Lassiter was the first IMB Missionary to the Aukan People. As he developed his strategy to reach the people group, he decided Chronological Bible Storying was the best method to present the gospel to them. He then noticed how spread out and transient they are. This was going make it very difficult to present the 40 stories that were chosen to present them the gospel. This is when Terry came up with the idea to put a Radio up to

transmit the Bible stories. The idea started off small and then grew. Terry was traveling back and forth from the city to the jungle working with the Aukaners. Terry was looking for a young couple to come and live among the people for longer periods of time. Charles and Brittany Shirey filled this request. When Charles arrived Terry told him about the radio project and how Charles would be heading up the project in the interior. Terry and Charles worked side by side for two years to complete this project. When it was finished there was a three hundred foot tower built on a two thousand foot mountain in the remote jungle. The studio is located nine miles from the tower in the village of Diitabiki. The studio is equipped with a seventy-five foot tower. We use a Studio Transmitter Link to transmit from the village studio to the remote mountain tower. Then from the tower we transmit out on a 250 watt FM transmitter. We are getting reports that tower is propagating over 100 miles.

Current status? Where aired? The radio has been in operation for nine years now. The radio is owned and run by a local board of Aukaners. It is operated from 5:00 p.m. to 11:00 p.m. every day. This is due to the power needs of the remote tower and the times when people are most available to hear the broadcast. The radio's typical schedule is from 5-7 they play songs and send out messages that people pay for, from 7-8 is the Bible hour when we play our Bible stories and other Christian songs or broadcast, from 8-9 is death announcements and village news, from 9-11 is Suriname and World news and any advertisements that they have. The radio station has a very strong following and has definitely become a lifeline along the river.

Follow-Up We do not use the radio as an end product. It is just part of our strategy to reach the Aukan people. The radio is the pre-evanglism tool that we use. Then we go into the villages and share the gospel one on one with the people. But now they have background knowledge that we can use in sharing with them. We have seen people come to know the Lord through the radio station, but more than anything it has helped so many people obtain a background about who God is and how He sent His son Jesus to this world to pay for our sins and show us the path to God.

Discussion Questions

Several of the missionary radio organizations (HCJB, TWR, FEBC/A) have realized that short wave is not effective in most places. For example, FEBC ceased short wave transmissions in the Thai language in 1983 and concentrated on local broadcasting on existing stations throughout Thailand with considerable impact. It is only in 2010/11 that they have begun broadcasting on their own community ststion in Bangkok.

Generally, there has been a move to establishing local station partnerships. This is discussed in the Radio/Audio Case 6. Most of these groups only provide the equipment and engineering to establish the station but not the programming. The Ankan station was developed separately with funds from the International Mission Board.

How can you help develop more effective radio programming that will reach the target people? Could you train them to write scripts, help them do research, etc.

FMI: Kevin G - kevingill@me.com

Radio/Audio Case 8: Worship Tape

Category: Music
Location: Kenya

For many years Christians in Kenya had only recordings of Church Choirs for entertainment. Most of these were recorded in the church because of the size of these choirs.

There was no need for the extra expense of the recording process, as the audience was just glad to get access to music that would lift their spirits. The majority of these cassettes were duplicated by a ministry associated with the African Inland Church, called Maturity Audio Visuals. This ministry (See Case 20- Mobile Vans in Africa) sold the tapes to raise money. The other main studio, Baptist Communication, was large enough to accommodate a choir, but many groups did not want to spend the extra money. The market started to change in the 1990s as some churches started to have worship groups like we see today. One such church was NC, which had a gifted worship leader and a good group. There seemed to be a market but the church did not have the capital for recording sessions.

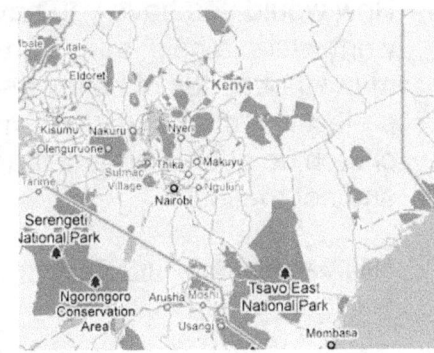

After a series of conversations with the pastor we decided to partner with NC and a talented Kenyan singer and composer and set up to record a live worship session at the church on a Friday night. Problems arose as we only had a 4 channel mixer, since the 8 channel one we had tried to borrow was not available. The other equipment we rented and the session was recorded. The leader was brought to his studio to record her voice and after a month we released *Melele Shukrani* (*Thanks for Life*), capitalized by what became CRI in Asia. The agreement was that the church would get a good percentage of the sale of the tapes. CRI would capitalize and manage duplicates and market the tape through the cinema van networks and other outlets in Nairobi. Problems arose as we did not have a written agreement with NC or the recordist. This created problems after the first 6 months as sales were excellant. NC thought CRI was getting "rich" and we had not even broken even on equipment rental (under $500)!

Successes

Even with this frustration, we still believe that it worked, as NC decided to do their next worship tape without our involvement!

Discussion Questions

How would you have you have approached this project? Is it worthwhile to help launch an industry that would minister to many thousands of believers? What priority would you give a project like this? Is it worthwhile to help the established church do such a project that mostly ministers to believers and not the lost?

FMI: Dan Henrich - info@comresources.org

Radio/Audio Case 9
UPG Radio Programming

Category: Shortwave radio
Location: China N PG UPG

CM Radio is a heart language, evangelistic radio broadcast that airs every night over short-wave radio over Trans World Radio. The goal is to use radio and other audio media formats to bring the gospel and the kingdom to the primarily non-literate N people group.

Synopsis

Each program has an announcer who welcomes and blesses the audience in the beginning as well as reviews the last program and introduces the program topic. Then the program switches to a fictional village setting where an uncle and nephew discuss happenings in the village. The uncle tells a Bible story relating to something going on in the village while the nephew voices the questions of the audience about the story from a non-believer (and in later broadcasts a new believer) perspective. The program also includes N PG praise songs, Christian testimonies, and a 1

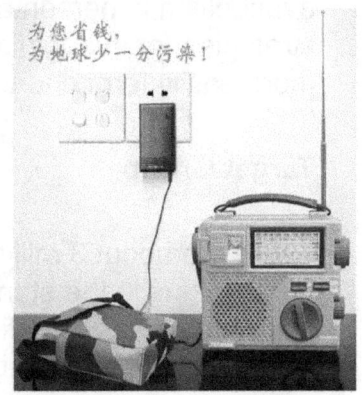

minute teaching point where the announcer reviews the story and answers the questions: What does the Bible story teach? How do you obey?

The guiding values for each program are that it should be: simple, concrete--not abstract, encourages reproduction of the message through using stories and songs, relevant--real questions by real people/not culturally offensive, God-centered--points to Jesus as the Lord and Savior, and Bible content.

Strategic Objective

The strategic objective is evangelistic seed sowing. We follow the principle of radio being effective for certain areas of the Engel's Scale. It is most effective for wide seed sowing at bringing someone from the point on the scale of little to knowledge about Jesus to the point of understanding God and the message of salvation. It is also effective for new believers understanding how to grow closer to God through basic discipleship and Biblical knowledge. However, radio is not the most effective form at the center of the scale where someone actually places their trust in Christ. The most effective form for this is one-on-one evangelism; therefore, we encourage our partners to do much evangelism in person and even combine these two strategies for evangelistic listening groups which can even more easily form churches.

Target Group

There are about 3 million N People Group in East Asia. The broadcast is in the standard SN dialect which about 1.5 to 2 million speak as their first language. The majority of people in the other 3 N PG subgroups can understand the broadcast also. The N PG are animistic and live primarily as subsistence farmers in the rural mountains of about 17 counties.

Estimated Audience

The estimated audience is unknown but is in the thousands with listeners that are non-Christians, Christians, and the numerous and problematic quasi-Christian Disciples Cult. At least one church has been formed from a group that was originally a non-Christian listening group where a Christian N PG was using the radio for evangelism.

How was it produced?

Several groups of GCC's have come together to produce this broadcast. These international folks have found the funding, determine series topics and Bible stories, and train the nationals. Christian N PG are the writers, voices, song writers, and do the recording. More and more of the work gets turned over to the N PG. The broadcast is produced in-country, sent out to TWR in Singapore, and then broadcast back in over short-wave radio from Guam.

Some of the research that was done included ethnographic research (for cultural relativity, bridges, barriers, and gaps), linguistic dialects (which areas and groups can understand the broadcast dialect), media form appropriateness, how to write and record a radio broadcast, chronological Bible storying strategies, which technical equipment to purchase, ethnomusicology, how to survey for analysis of effective communication, and how to strategic follow-up.

Current Status

The broadcast has been airing 15 minutes every night since July 1, 2008. There have been a couple of series with 40+ episodes covering the entire Bible. Other series include series on Abraham, Proverbs, the life and teachings of Jesus, and discipleship. Every other week the entire Creation to Christ fast track story is broadcast. Other forms of media for giving people the broadcast content include mp3 players, the Saber hand-crank player, the MegaVoice solar player, and CD's. The songs have also been popularly received as CD's with many people enjoying a DVD karaoke of people doing traditional style dances to the praise songs. About 35 episodes have been translated and recorded into the BN N PG sub-dialect and handed out on mp3 players.

Reaching the N People Group—8 Lessons We've Learned:

God is sending people from all around the world to reach the N PG. With a new evangelistic broadcast, our aim is for the N PG to hear His good news of salvation loudly and clearly. I want to share with you 8 lessons our team has learned over the past couple of years. Most of these lessons have to do with issues that can also apply to your own ministry whether at home or abroad.

1. **Heart Language Is Our Biggest Spiritual Bridge.** The N PG are animists that appeal to shamans and sacrifices to appease spirits that harm the N PG through curses and diseases. Animal sacrifices are performed at all the big events--births, funerals, weddings, the building of a house, a new job, a new year. The shamans, called bimos, will also cast spirits into a person called a suni. When these sunis are fully possessed they have great spiritual power for

predicting the future and healing sicknesses. All these are ways the N PG attempt to find a way out of bondage and fear.

Currently less than 1% of the N PG are Christians. Sometimes you will see different numbers here, but it is difficult to count due to both the restricting laws over Christianity and some dangerous quasi-Christian cults that are already throughout the mountains.

While a lot of the men are able to speak Chinese, most of the older people, women, and children under 12 can not speak Chinese and most people are illiterate. Even some of the most educated N PG I know are still primary oral learners. Radio airwaves can cross into all the high mountain villages where the N PG live in their mud homes in poverty. Unless the N PG that live in the mountains can afford a VCD player, there are almost no other options for them to hear any media in their language other than the government's radio broadcast of the news.

When you go into a N PG village, people tend to look at you very stone-faced wondering why you are there. If you greet them in the national language they will grin and nod at you in a friendly manner. But when you use their own language to greet them, they break out in huge smiles and eagerly start talking with you. And if it's at all close to one of the 2 times of day they eat their meals, they will invite you back to their house to roast potatoes in the coals of their fire pit or kill a chicken to make a delicious chicken soup. Like most minority groups in this country, they are looked down upon by the majority group, but when anyone actually honors them by using their own language, it is an automatic bridge to friendship.

Here's an example of the effects of people hearing something in their heart language. My majority group friend had been teaching some N PG Christians in Chinese for a long time and they had often sung Chinese praise songs. But when he let them listen to a recording of the first N PG praise song they had ever heard, the N PG Christians began to sing it over and over and over with such a joy he had never heard them sing the Chinese praise songs.

When we are out promoting the broadcast, we can easily gather a group of people together by singing N PG songs or playing the radio broadcast over some speakers. The N PG are attracted to media in their own heart language

We *must* put the gospel truth in a context and heart language that people can truly understand.

(Q—What is the biggest spiritual bridge to reaching the audience you are ministering to?)

Members of the Body of Christ must use their giftings to work together with others. Perhaps this is the biggest lesson that our radio team has learned. It's the biggest lesson that I'd like to get across to you. We *must* work together to reach the world. We *must* work together to reach the N PG.

When our team first came together in May of 2006, it was a discovery meeting called together by an international worker asking anyone who was interested to come to the meeting. There were people from diverse organizations with very diverse strategies for reaching the N PG. We were also folks who were already busy and committed to different approaches for reaching the N PG with some people focusing on language and translation, some on community development, and others on trying to start reproducing churches.

By our second meeting we were unified in purpose that an evangelistic broadcast could reach the N PG, *but* because we were so different we could not even agree on how much of the gospel should be shared in a 15 minute broadcast.

This problem mostly had to do with our preconceptions about our fellow workers' intentions. As we discussed the term "evangelistic broadcast" we formed into 2 different sides of discussion. One side perceived the other side to be saying that each broadcast should ask people to repeat a prayer at the end of each radio program and this prayer would work like magic to save them forever so long as they merely said the words. That was not what the group was saying, but that's how it was perceived. The other side perceived the other group to say that an evangelistic broadcast was merely about community development. That's not what that group was really saying either. This important second meeting could be described as a little heated. It wasn't until the next meeting that we understood our problem was our preconceptions of the other workers because of their organizations and methodologies. We found out we all actually agreed that we wanted the evangelical story of the Bible to be clearly presented.

The beautiful part of this whole thing came in our first year of production. None of us could commit to doing this full-time so we each pitched in as we could. Everybody contributed according to their gifting with some people focusing on raising financial support, others on the organization of writing and recording, some people serving to arrange logisitics for recording session, some musical people focused on helping people write praise songs, and others helped in technology by learning how to purchase and use the right recording equipment. We had many international workers doing their part and many national workers doing their part. Of course it's the N PG believers who are the writers, the voices, the song writers, the singers, the back translators, and the ones recording their true testimonies. But we also can't forget the fellowships in both North America and Asia contributing financially and advising us.

July 1, 2008, a year and a half from our first production meeting, we went on the air with a nightly 15 minute broadcast.   We have lived out Romans 12.4-8, *"For as in one body we have many members, and the members do not all have the same function, so we, though many, are one body in Christ, and individually members one of another. Having gifts that differ according to the grace given to us, let us use them: if prophecy, in proportion to our faith; if service, in our serving; the one who teaches, in his teaching; the one who exhorts in his exhortation; the one who contributes, in generosity; the one who leads, with zeal; the one who does acts of mercy, with cheerfulness."*

In everything you hear from me today hear this: it's going to take the members of the body of Christ around the world using their giftings and callings to work together to reach the N PG.

(Q—Are you using your gifts in your ministry and cooperating well with others who are using different gifts and callings?)

Storying Is an effective method. Our main content centers around Bible stories. Bible stories are interesting, they're easy to memorize and retell, and stories are concrete which is how non-literate people to learn the best. There's a great quote used in the introduction of every Story4all podcast,

"75% of the Bible is stories and 70% of the world is oral. Aren't we missing something?" The N PG love stories and the Bible teaches most of its truth through stories so that's what we try to do with the broadcast.

We used the Following Jesus method to craft 2 chronological story sets of 45 stories each. We used stories that told the big picture of the Bible as well as specific stories that helped speak to cultural bridges and cultural barriers to the gospel. We also have a third series of 45 episodes on the life and teachings of Jesus.

We have had multiple examples of people taking an entire series of 45 of the 15 minute episodes out to groups of unbelievers who enjoyed listening to episode after episode until they finished the entire set. One time an entire clan was meeting together for about a week to help decide what to do when a couple wanted to get a divorce. Since they were sitting around most of the time one of our partners gave them 45 of the episodes to listen to and most of them listened to the entire series and planned to continue listening to the broadcast.

Another time an international worker had been going to a village and eventually 2 N PG became believers. A few months later, one of the believers died in a flood. One day when the international worker went to see the other believer in the village, people in the village just stayed in their houses. Finally a few men came out and told him to leave. They said the other believer had died and they didn't want the international worker to come back. They began to start throwing rocks at him until he left.

The worker was quite upset about both of his friends dying and the villagers throwing rocks at him. The village seemed to be strongly in the grip of Satan. Later the worker asked a N PG believer from another area to go to the village and find out what was really going on. The N PG believer had a small mp3 player with 90 episodes of an evangelistic broadcast in the NY language so he purchased a small set of speakers from the store and set out for the village.

After a little while in the village the believer soon found out he had a few cousins there that he had never known about. Over the course of several days visiting in the village 25 people listened to all 90 episodes of the radio program. This means that they were able to hear N PG praise songs, N PG testimonies, and 2 chronological Bible storying presentations. No one put their trust in Christ at the time, but in that once hostile village, the gospel was shared boldly and clearly through the medium of the mp3 player. The N PG believer will be going back there very soon.

(Q—How much of the Bible teaching in your ministry reflects the 75% of the Bible that is stories?)

Song writing workshops are catalysts. I can't say enough about the power of songs and song writing. Songs of praising God are a major attraction to our broadcast, but we chose to keep song writing separate from our radio project for security reasons and to bring more N PG Christians from different networks together. We began with one workshop to teach a few people about song writing and give them an opportunity to write a song together. Soon there were other workshops with more people with more songs being written each time. One time about a week after a song was written, one of the participants heard the song being sung in the train station about a 10 hour train ride away.

In just over a year songs were polished and recorded and the first N PG praise CD of 20 songs was produced. We have also recorded a second CD of 14 more songs that include not only praise songs, but Christmas songs, a wedding song, children songs, and funeral songs. Even more exciting is that a group of young N PG believers that have been part of this song writing and recording formed an informal band and are hoping to produce their own CD of more songs this summer. The N PG are writing their own hymnal and building relationships with other Christians outside of their own hc and hc network.

One of our partners took the songs to play for a family he was visiting. Later when he went outside he heard people singing the one of the songs that was playing inside earlier.

When a N PG believer who lived far away in the provincial capital heard the N PG praise songs for the first time her response was, "I didn't think any other N PG Christians were doing anything, but now I know they are. I have to give a copy of this to my mother and father."

Song writing workshops catalyze indigenous hymn writing, unity among N PG believers, music for CD's and the radio, and self-ownership of reaching the N PG.

(Q—Have you tried the both easy and exciting exercise of song writing with the people whom you minister to?)

Use multiple teaching methods. In our broadcast we proclaim the gospel through Bible stories, brief teaching application points, praise songs, and true testimonies of N PG believers. Within the broadcast the Bible story is told by a respected Uncle in a fictional village setting. We use this ongoing village storyline and dialogue to bridge from the life and culture of the N PG to the gospel.

As we use this village storyline method we are also *modeling*. We are modeling the effects of the gospel, how people should do evangelism, how people live godly and transformed lives as they react to various situations, dialogue with unbelievers, and get baptized.

Jesus used multiple teaching methods and so should we.

(Q—Think of one of your ministry projects. How many teaching methods do you use and could you use more?

Intentionally form listening groups. The Engel's Scale is an attempt to describe someone's spiritual journey from a point of no knowledge of God to spiritual maturity.

People generally move from the top of no awareness of a supreme being (-8) down through a growing knowledge of the gospel to the stage of knowing they need to make a decision (-2) and actual repentance and faith in Jesus Christ (-1) until they are changed as new beings (0). Significant growth points such as prayer, joining a church fellowship, evangelism are represented by the continued downward movement into the positive points of the scale.

Radio is effective at bringing many people from the point of no knowledge of God to a point of clearly understanding the gospel. It's also effective at bringing many new Christians to a point of spiritual maturity. However, radio is least effective at actually helping people cross the point on the Engel's scale where they actually put their trust in Christ as their Savior. The most effective means of communication at that point is face-to-face communication, which is represented on this graph as visitation. Face-to-face, however, is not as *efficient* at bringing *the masses* of people from the point of no knowledge of God to a point of clearly understanding the gospel or bringing *masses* of new Christians to the point of spiritual maturity. Evangelism by radio and evangelism by visitation must go together.

All this is to say evangelistic radio ministry, even with good content, is only as good as the follow-up. In our case about the only follow-up you can do is face-to-face.

We have learned from many effective radio ministries around the world that forming evangelistic listening groups can lead to churches. The ministry Faith Comes by Hearing has used this effectively when in 2006 they used the J-film to share Christ and started listening groups by challenging them to a commitment of listening to the program 30 minutes at a time twice a week. If people committed, they left an audio player with them with the NT in their heart language. They started these listening groups in 501 places in mostly restricted access countries and had a goal of retaining 80% of the listening groups. Within 6 months they had lost only 4 of the 501 listening groups, they had 27,000 regular listeners, and 350 of those groups had become churches.

Many people on our team are trying to do the same kind of thing by training people to start evangelistic listening groups and discuss the topics among themselves. We train people using a story that has a model of 2 believers singing N PG praise songs to form a bridge of a relationship and sharing the gospel so that by the end of the night they have challenged a group of gathered people in a village to start a listening group. The believers' church is also a part because they're the ones who took up an offering to purchase the radio as a gift and are the ones praying for the group to put their trust in Jesus.

The N PG need groups of believers instead of believers living in isolation from one another. Forming listening groups is an easy way for our partners to be intentional and effective at face-to-face follow-up.

(Q—Do you and your partners intentionally use an effective method of grouping interested individuals together?)

Focus on audio content not just the medium of radio broadcasts. Yes, radio broadcasting is the quickest and farthest reaching medium to reach the most people but we can also put the content on CD's, mp3 players, MegaVoice Ambassador solar players, and Saber hand-crank players. Using audio players is also a simple way for grouping people to share with them. We try to focus on producing the content and putting it in any form that is strategic for our partners to use in their own ministry.

There's even a story about the NG praise songs spreading at the mobile phone office when people standing nearby liked the songs being transferred onto a believer's cell phone as a ringtone. The mobile phone office kept the songs for themselves as well.

One time we loaded up the Saber player with 20 NY praise songs, 5 evangelistic broadcasts, and an audio file that tells you the frequency and schedule of the broadcast. Before this, we used a method of promotion where non-N PG speaking backpackers would come and give radios to people along with cards telling people the frequency, but of course many people cannot read. They usually gave radios away inside households.

This time a group would start playing songs when they got close to a N PG village and groups of 30-50 would very soon gather around. Then they would hand them a radio and play the audio file explaining how to tune in. They played it several times until they were sure people understood.

This method worked much better than the original method because people would often sit together and listen to the 5 episodes over and over. One time people listened to the songs and announcement and then left while the group ate supper at one of the houses. Then just before the program came on at 8, the house where they were eating filled up with people all eager to listen to the broadcast together. When they left the next morning, some folks from the village gathered as the group departed and sang some of the praise songs to them that they had learned by listening to the Saber the night before.

The Saber is useful for crossing language barriers and for gathering groups that cross household boundaries. Sabers can help form listening groups and daily radio broadcasts can help listening groups become regular listening groups with new content.

(Q—Are you using media in the most strategic way possible so that churches can be started?)

Technology pays off. In the past few years we've distributed about 800 radios with about 150 of these being distributed by one of the N PG hc networks. Several new churches with leaders that have been Christians less than a year are using the radio to learn from the Word each day. A N PG hc network that has been around for a while identified about 20 places that they were going to use radios to start evangelistic listening groups. An older lady, a new believer, who could not speak the majority well was being discipled by someone in the majority language. Later when this lady began to listen to the broadcast, the person discipling her began to notice a big change in her spiritual growth and she started sharing the gospel with many people.

Yes, radio costs a lot of money. But if it is used effectively and attractively—with the right content, the right teaching methods, the right language, the right promotion, and the right follow-up—churches can pop up all over the mountains where the N PG live. As our team mission statement says, we "can share the gospel of Christ in order to promote a full Christian life and community in local bodies so the kingdom of God is established among the N PG." With its *exponentially multiplying effect on other types of ministry*, radio can reach the nearly 3 million N PG. That's a lot of people, but it's certainly doable. And it's going to take the members of the body of Christ around the world using their giftings and callings to work together to reach the N PG. God works through the body of believers.

Radio is a method that each of us can use to cross almost any barrier that exists between the N PG and their understanding of the gospel.

Radio/Audio Case 10:

UPG Radio Programming

Category: Shortwave radio
Location: East Asia - KT

In order to spread the Gospel among KT People Group in their heart language, there is a daily 30-minute Christian broadcast originating from the Philippines in their language.

Strategic Objective

To get the gospel to a remote UPG group in the high mountains Asia.

Area of its Use (target group):

KT of East Asia

Estimated Audience

The estimated total KT population is 1.7 million. The estimated number of KT that have access to the broadcast is between 50,000 to 75,000 based on surveys done by volunteer teams and the number of radios passed out over the years.

How was it produced?

The FEBC (Far East Broadcasting Company) broadcast was produced in conjunction with several partners, including

Christian partners. We work with a key W partner who is doing most of the production with the help of KT Christians. The only research was frequency testing to determine if the radio signal could reach into KT areas. We worked together as a team to determine the best content for the daily programming.

Current status? Where aired?

The broadcast currently airs daily from 9:00 pm to 9:30 pm. The program has been on the air for the past seven years and is broadcast from an FEBC short-wave antennas in Manila.

Follow-Up

Follow-up has been an issue we are working on because the areas that we distribute radios to are very nomadic. Very rarely do these people stay in one place from year to year. The areas we distribute to are very remote. We intentionally picked those areas because they have very little chance if any to be exposed to the gospel.

Discussion

How could this format be improved? Take a look again at Radio/Audio Case 9 and see what could be adapted to fit to this outreach.

What information is missing from this? Is there a way to learn more from the results without technology?

Radio/Audio Case 11:

Faith Comes by Hearing Partnership case with Campus Crusade for Christ

The JESUS Film has proven to be one of the greatest tools for evangelism. Many different missions' organizations and churches use The JESUS Film in partnership with Campus Crusade, including **Faith Comes By Hearing**. *The listening programs of* **Faith Comes By Hearing** *provide a follow-up tool for discipleship after the JESUS Film showings are conducted.*

PARTNERSHIP HISTORY

Faith Comes By Hearing's partnership with Campus Crusade was birthed from conversations with Paul Eshleman, who after showing Morgan Jackson the impact of the film, also explained that most of the people coming to Christ are non-literate, which makes following up the film with discipleship very difficult. He requested the assistance of Faith Comes By Hearing to help solve this problem, initiating a powerful move of God to reach people who need to hear the message of Jesus and be discipled by His Word.

These ministries partner tested the project in India, proving that the combination of The *JESUS* Film with Faith Comes By Hearing was truly an incredible way to evangelize and disciple poor and non-literate people in their own heart languages.

PARTNERSHIP PROGRAMS

The *JESUS* Film Project and Faith Comes By Hearing assembled teams that worked together using national workers who live in the area where the film was shown. This enables the FCBH team to conduct follow-up to the film using local transportation.

The *JESUS* Film team works with local church leaders so that when a showing has been done, there is a pastor or several church workers available to follow up the "New Life Group" that is formed after the showing.

The following is the process that was used during a "pilot" with JESUS Film several years ago. The final "data" is presented in another document. Since then, there have been other models used with great success depending on the infrastructure being used by the partnering organization:

1. On the day that the *JESUS* Film is to be shown, the FCBH teams go to the villages with a church worker. They play the Gospel of Mark to different groups of people, looking for a "man or woman of peace." This is a person who is impacted by what they hear and becomes willing to host the FCBH listening group. As the team goes through the village, they make people aware of the *JESUS* Film showing that evening.

2. When the *JESUS* Film has been shown and the invitation to accept Christ has been given, then those who have come to Christ and even those who have not, but want to learn more, are invited to come

together weekly with the hosting man or woman of peace to listen to the dramatized New Testament at an appointed time.

3. The church worker then returns at the appointed time to listen with the people in the "New Life Group." The listening is normally about 30 minutes long, followed by a time for questions, discussion, and prayer. The section of Scripture heard is often repeated several times since oral people want to hear stories over and over again, memorizing the Scriptures.

4. The New Testament is presented on the Proclaimer which is given to the group leader. They are encouraged to come together to listen as often as they want.

5. One of the FCBH workers visits the group on their first meeting and then returns once a month for the next six months. These visits are to encourage the church worker to continue to follow up and to document the number of listeners and transformation of lives and communities.

6. At the end of six months, the New Life Group is left in the hands of the church worker and the FCBH worker moves on to another new group formed in the area. Each FCBH worker can follow up on 25 Christ Groups at a time and work with 50 groups in a year. So a team of two workers can follow 100 showings of the JESUS Film.

Using this system, a New Life Group can be formed in almost every village where the JESUS Film has been shown. Experience demonstrates that after six months, 20 percent of these groups, for a variety of reasons, will have fallen away. But the groups that remain will grow and average about 35 listeners at six months and will still continue growing.

In oral communities, people like to gather together for discussions and communal decisions. Oral people do not separate themselves from a story, and so when they hear the New Testament, they enter the story in their minds, and to them it is like they are there, experiencing what they hear. Many are healed, delivered and receive miraculous provision from prayer requests. These experiences make the Scriptures real to them and cause groups to make corporate decisions for Christ -- baptism, removal of idols, separation from immorality and churches are formed.

Since most are non-literate, they want to hear the same story, parable or teaching over and over again in an effort to memorize. They do not believe they "own" it unless they have it memorized. The time of questions and answers after each session is where heart and life issues are exposed and answers found together. Although the church worker will answer many questions, most answers are found from among the group as they discuss what the Bible says.

The basic discipleship model is people hearing the whole of the New Testament repeatedly over a period of one year. Then they discuss and ask questions, understanding what they have heard and memorizing much of the Scriptures. Having the church worker in their presence makes certain that the Christ Group is connected to a church and has access to Christian leaders. The church worker can go to their church for help in answering questions and can bring other believers who can help in developing Christian worship.
FMI: Doug Harstine <DHarstine@fcbhmail.org>

Radio/Audio Case 12:

Using Audio Bibles to Make Disciples in Oral Cultures:

Viability, reproducibility, and long term results.

Introduction

I (Greg Fisher) come to this study with 21 years of experience working and living in Africa. My earliest assignment as an apprentice missionary was to design and implement non-formal extension training programs for pastors in West Africa.   This was my first experience of working in an oral culture; however, at that time we did not understand the problem as one of orality. We were looking at difficulties as cultural challenges of which lack of literacy was simply one of many challenges to be surmounted.

It was only as I came to serve as the Regional Manager for Africa for Hosanna/Faith Comes By Hearing in 2006 that I was introduced to the concept of Orality. I was very intrigued by the challenge of discipleship in oral cultures, and interested in the Faith Comes By Hearing (FCBH) audio scripture listening program as a possible strategy for making disciples using the Proclaimer[2] as a tool.

Why We Did This Research

Like all of you with any sort of mission field experience, I have to admit that I came to Hosanna/Faith Comes By Hearing with some questions. The story of Hosanna and FCBH was intriguing. My first meetings with Morgan Jackson, Hosanna's International Director, inspired me to believe that FCBH could be a viable approach to reaching oral communities with the scriptures in the heart language of the listeners. My first field visits to FCBH programs in Africa were challenging to me. I saw the FCBH program in action, and I could see the real possibilities of FCBH as a strategy for discipleship. I also realized that not every group I visited was using the strategy as effectively as they could have.

As I continued to work with FCBH I became aware of anecdotal reporting that seemed to bear out my hoped for conclusion that most generally the FCBH programs were working. But, I also had some serious questions that needed answering:

1. What results would I find 6 months after a group had started listening? Would the FCBH group still be functional? Or, would it have died?

2. Was the FCBH approach simply a source of entertainment in a village where entertainment resources were in short supply? Or, would listening to the audio scriptures actually make a positive impact on community attitudes and practices?

3. Was FCBH simply imposing yet another western made solution on an African problem? Or, could FCBH be flexible enough to blend into the local context? What would that look like?

4. Dr. Don McGregor, my old mentor, used to hammer into our heads the need for infinite reproducibility of anything we introduced into the field. Was FCBH reproducible? Could it propagate itself on the field without inputs of direction and support from the West? Or, had we constructed yet another program of infinite dependency?

5. How could I get the answers to these questions without finding my desk stacked with hand questionnaires filled out in a manner to please "the expert from afar"?

Research Methodology

Once when I was passing through the airport security lines at Johannesburg, South Africa I was asked by the security person, "Is there anything in your carry-on that you are unaware of?" It is an impossible question to answer! It is obvious that I can only be aware of what I am aware of! It is similarly true when it came to FCBH. I was only aware of what I was aware of, with no real ideas about how to find out what I was unaware of. So, how should we approach our field research? We could go into the field with pre-determined questions, but the end result might be simply a verification of what we already knew. While that is important, it doesn't tell us what we are unaware of about FCBH as a strategy and The Proclaimer as a tool for the discipleship of oral cultures.

Confused? So was I. I needed hard data that I hoped would demonstrate the effectiveness of FCBH, but it was difficult to decide where to start asking the questions. After some thought we settled on using an unusual methodology called *Grounded Theory Research*[3]. This is a research methodology pioneered in the 1960's by two sociologists from the University of California-Berkley, Barney Glaser and Anselm Strauss, who were collaborating in research on dying hospital patients. Since—as far as they knew—no one had ever experienced death and come back to report on the experience, they had to pioneer a new methodology that would be accepted in the academic community to do this study. The strength of using *Grounded Theory* is that our hypotheses and eventually our theories come from the ground up, rather than from our literature review down to the ground. This approach is commonly used as a research methodology in the social sciences where qualitative data is equally valued with quantitative data. *Grounded Theory* seemed a better fit with my own operational methodology as well as giving us an opportunity to hear directly from FCBH end users in the field. Our goal was, insofar as possible, to view FCBH through the lens of the end user. We understood, of course, that some biases from our field researchers would certainly be visible in the data.

Non-Participant Observers

To accomplish our research we would need trained non-participant observers to go out and see FCBH in action within the context of Africa. Using Westerners as non-participant observers was ruled out immediately for the obvious reasons of cultural bias and language difficulties. The non-participant observers were to observe actual FCBH programs without entering into the program or participating in the discussion—until after the FCBH group listening activity was finished. They could then ask questions of the participants, group leaders, partner representatives, and community observers. They would record the answers, and make field notes on each group.

Hosanna maintains four field coordinators in Africa. These four are African nationals, who, with the exception of one, hold Baccalaureate degrees or higher from recognized African universities. We spent three days during our annual field coordinators meetings to train them to be non-participant observers of FCBH groups. Our initial field research forms had two sections: A quantitative data section and a qualitative data section. We practiced with our coordinators asking open-ended questions, without making them to be leading questions which might suggest to our respondents the answer we were looking for. We hoped using these methods would lead coordinators—and us—to both answers and further qualitative questions. We also trained our field coordinators to be keen observers of group behavior and to ask lots of questions about group behaviors and community observations not included on the initial form.

An official e-mail was sent to the head of each of our partner organizations explaining that Hosanna was undertaking to do post-project verification research which we called "Rice Checking". We called this research "Rice Checking" because the name made it seem less threatening, and, it gave us an opportunity to explain that we wanted only to check a few of the groups, in much the same manner as one would check the doneness of cooked rice. Each organization was informed that this would be used as research to verify the results of FCBH to our donors. It was explained in that e-mail that our field coordinator would need unhindered access to the records of the FCBH project for the purpose of selecting a random sample. Each coordinator would also have an e-mail from me outlining the size of the sample and suggesting the mix of implementing partners and languages that was deemed to be of interest to our study. Each researcher would select the random sample directly from our partner's records and once the sample was pulled, no group could be removed from the sample. These samples were selected outside the presence of the partner doing the FCBH program. This was done to avoid a partner filling the random sample with only known successful groups (i.e. the "FCBH show groups" that might be common showcase programs for visitors). Regardless of what the researcher found, they were required to do a full report on each group in the sample. We expected to find groups that had failed to take off or were inactive for some reason. At this point we didn't know all the reasons a group might fail, so finding this information was as valuable to us as finding an active group. If an FCBH group was inactive, and wasn't meeting for temporary or permanent reasons, that information as well as the reasons for the failure were noted as well. The forms used for field notes by our researchers were all completed in handwritten form. This was to avoid the temptation to simply cut and paste reoccurring answers onto the forms.

As the data was received, my Albuquerque staff[4] did an initial review of the results. Some data was obviously not correct. In two cases it was very obvious that the partner had manipulated our field researcher and tainted the random sample selection process. This was apparent because these were the only two programs in all of Africa to be one hundred percent successful in all respects with no inactive groups. In those cases the data was removed from our research results and do not appear in our research data base. All data was seriously challenged by all of us as we received it. Any data that seemed suspicious to us in any way was closely questioned and—in some cases—referred back to our field researcher for further clarification.

The Barney Glaser dictum of "everything is data" was drummed into our researcher's heads. Photographs are data. Side comments you overhear from the group leader are data. Your own observations of the group, guided by your own experience, are data. The testimonies of people whose lives have been impacted by the FCBH audio scripture listening program are data. Complaints about FCBH from pastors, group leaders, and community leaders are data. Everything is data. Glaser also makes an important statement to further clarify what is data:

> "There are apparently at least four types of data. First is baseline, which is the best description a participant can offer. The second is properline[5]data, which is what the participant thinks is proper to tell the researcher. It is what the participants feel they are supposed to say, no matter what reality is. They have no stake

in correct description, only in correct distortion. The third is <u>interpreted</u> data, which is what is told by a trained professional whose job it is to make sure that others see the data in his professional way, despite the fact that it alters the normal way of seeing it …. The fourth type of data is <u>vaguing out</u>. There is no stake for the participant in telling the researching anything, so he just vagues out."[6]

Our research began in April 2009, and the initial results presented in this paper required 17 months of work.[7] In order to avoid having our conclusions skewed by regional bias, the sample groups were taken from the West, East, Southern, and Horn of Africa. Thirteen partner programs were researched in 10 countries.[8] This required 178 days of in the field work by our researchers. We currently have a data base of 318 randomly selected groups in our field data. Each of these groups in the random sample were personally visited and observed by our field researchers.

During the early fall of 2010 I began having meetings with my staff to discuss ways of moving into the next step of our research: Coding the data. My two assistants and I began reading over every individual field note, narrative report, photograph, every shred of data. The documents were read and re-read dozens of times over a two month period. Finally patterns of information began to emerge from the data. These were the patterns of information we had hoped to find. It was information about what we didn't know about FCBH as a field program and had been—up to that time—unable to formulate the questions to ask. (We will return to the detail of these patterns at a later point in this paper). We listed every pattern that we could see emerging— eventually 181 patterns emerged—and, they fell into 12 categories. Each of the patterns of information was challenged by other members of the Albuquerque group. Some patterns we initially thought we saw were later found to be our own bias imposed on the research. The challenging process helped us to eliminate most (but, not all) of our own biases from our research and allow the data to speak directly to us. From these emerging patterns we made a coding sheet that gave a numeric index number to each of the patterns of information. The data was re-read again and we coded our qualitative data using our coding sheet. This was intended to allow us to view FCBH through the lens of the end users. It allowed us to see what use they had made of our program; how they had contextualized it for their specific needs; and, what long term impacts they had experienced from using FCBH.

FCBH From The Perspective of Hosanna

Before looking at research outcomes and patterns of information, let us first understand clearly the program that Hosanna/FCBH introduced into the field context. We will later see some stark contrasts between what was introduced and what our partners eventually implemented in their context. This is a good problem to have, since it demonstrates the flexibility of the FCBH program.

Our Mission and Vision

Hosanna's vision is to bring God's Church together and make disciples. To accomplish this vision, we are committed to putting every translation of the Bible in audio form, and to implementing the Faith Comes

By Hearing audio scripture listening program in every church or village in the world. Our intention is that all people, especially the 50% of the world who cannot read, will be able to hear the New Testament in the language they use for prayer. So, the first step in accomplishing this task is the recording of the New Testament where ever there is a viable translation. At present FCBH offers 601 individual scripture recordings in 500 different languages. These are the heart languages of 5.0 billion people—or, more than 2/3 of the world's population. We are currently using FCBH as a discipleship tool for oral communities in 154 countries.[9] In Africa we have recorded more than 250 languages which we are using for FCBH in 33 countries.[10]

The challenges to Hosanna in accomplishing this task are formidable. As the chart above shows, of the 7 billion people living in the world 50% are non-literate. So, our challenge becomes providing an audio scripture recording in every language where an existing New Testament translation exists. This is not to exclude the validity of Chronological Bible Storytelling or other narrative methodologies, and in some cases Hosanna has worked with storytelling methodologies to produce recordings where no New Testament currently exists. However, our primary mission is to impact the lives of people with the audio scriptures and Hosanna places a high value on Bible translation. As Walter Ong mentions in his seminal work on orality and literacy:

> "In Christianity, for example, the Bible is read aloud at liturgical services. For God is thought of always as 'speaking' to human beings, not as writing to them. The orality of the mindset

in the Biblical text, even in its epistolary sections, is overwhelming … "[11]

Ong goes on to assert:

"In Trinitarian theology, the Second Person of the Godhead is the Word, and the human analogue for the Word here is not the human written word, but the human spoken word. God the father 'speaks' his Son: he does not inscribe him. Jesus, The Word of God, left nothing in writing, though he could read and write."[12]

So, our ministry model is based upon the foundation of Romans 10:17, "So then faith *cometh* by hearing and hearing by the word of God." As the chart above shows, the Faith Comes By Hearing audio Bible listening programs are established by working within the structures of existing partners. Our field coordinators in Africa are experienced in training partners to carry out the establishment of listening groups. Since FCBH places such an emphasis on scripture use and scripture engagement, we are not generally interested in mass distribution numbers. It is our commitment to scripture impact that has motivated this study. [13]

Our basic discipleship model is one of people hearing the whole of the New Testament by listening regularly over a one year period. After each listening session they conclude with discussion and ask questions, to facilitate understanding of what they have heard, as well as memorizing many of the stories—especially those found in the Gospels. As we will see later in this paper, the open discussion of the text following the listening is a vital key to the success of FCBH. The illustration that follows in the next section gives a pictorial model of the five elements of the FCBH program. These five elements are all based firmly upon the scriptures as the Word of God. Hosanna places a high value on the written text of the scriptures, and a high value on the scripture translation process. Where additional materials are introduced into the FCBH program, they are introduced by implementing partners in the field to help contextualize the program for their listeners.

Our FCBH program has five essential elements of design, which we call the Five Pillars of FCBH. These pillars, or essential design elements are:

1. **FCBH is a program of Bible listening.** While we are aware that not every person in every oral culture is non-literate, we have established that listening to the audio scriptures is an important element of our methodology. In actual practice the listening sessions with discussion, at times, closely resemble the kind of oral interaction that is common to oral communities. In addition, Hosanna has re-conceptualized the entire New Testament as a drama.[14] The 165 (or more) speakers in the New Testament are voiced by 25 people in the recording of the New Testament.[15] In addition, a sound track of dramatic sound effects and music is added to the field recordings in our post-recording studio editing. To say that Hosanna has re-conceptualized the New Testament as a drama does not mean that the recordings lack faithfulness to the written text of the New Testament

translation in anyway. Our initial thought in designing FCBH was that it would be a church based discipleship program. It would be a way for national Bible agencies to encourage scripture engagement in the church.

2. **FCBH is Bible listening in groups.** Our experience shows us that in oral cultures the participants engage more actively with the listening when it is done in groups. In addition, there is the added benefit of group accountability for what has been heard from the New Testament.

3. **Open discussion follows group listening.** The open discussion is fascinating to watch. The group has to wrestle with the meaning of the story as it applies to their own context. In some of the charts that follow this section you will see the perceived impacts of this group discussion as reported by our respondents in the field.

4. **Each group established must receive at least two follow-up visits.** Initially we conceived of this as holding the group accountable for its commitment to listen through the entire New Testament. It was also a way of re-enforcing the idea that the Proclaimer was placed into the village or church setting as community property and not individual property. However, as the data will prove, proper follow up of the groups serves as a much more vital aspect for the success of FCBH. The follow up

visits can be used to encourage the group to complete the listening as well as plant the seeds of group multiplication in the minds of the group listeners.

5. **Reporting back to Hosanna.** Since FCBH is made available through donor funding, the reporting back to Hosanna of the results along with testimonies of lives changed helps us to close the donor communication loop by reporting on specific FCBH projects as well as to improve the program for the future. At first we found reporting back to Hosanna a great challenge for some of our partners. More recently, our shift towards more post project verification research such as this study has helped us to close the donor communication loop with better and more factually verifiable information.

Answering the "so what?" question.

A viable research project must be able to answer the "so what?" question. So, what importance does this research have? What questions does it answer? What difference does it make that the research project was undertaken in the first place? Our questions that we went into the field to get answers to are as follows:

1. Would it be possible for us to view the FCBH program through the lens of the end user?

2. What use had the end user made of the FCBH program? We knew what

had been introduced into the field through our trainers, but, how had the program actually been used? In what interesting ways was it contextualized in different areas of Africa?

3. What long term impacts would the end users of the program report to our researchers? We knew the long term impacts we hoped to see; however, we wanted to know the impacts the end user reported to help us to measure impacts hoped for against actual impacts seen.

4. In addition to learning the impacts of FCBH on end users—persons— were there additional impacts on institutions like churches and schools as well? If so, what were these impacts?

A first look at both program line data and base line data.

2009 FCBH Impact in Africa

Out of the 26,771 Proclaimers sent...

An Additional 8,031 groups were formed

77,636 people gave their lives to Christ

48,187 people were baptized

3,694 Churches were planted

20,345 groups were still active after 7 months

Groups tend to listen to 2 chapters at a time

As we pointed out above, typically a mission organization is dealing with two distinct types of data:

144

Properline data (which our team has renamed programline data) and baseline data. From our earlier discussion it will be remembered that properline data is data in which the respondent tells the researcher what he thinks the researcher wants to hear; while baseline data is when the respondent gives the best and most accurate answer to the researcher. One of our first tasks was to compare the quantitative program line data reporting with our base line data from our random sample groups. What we found was that while there were obvious discrepancies between the two data types, our program line data did seem to mirror in many respects our baseline data. In one case a field partner used highly inflated results—programline data —for reporting back to Hosanna. This reporting would in no way mirror our baseline data from the research. Other partners, while using more reliable reporting, would fail to report on group failures or group multiplication. The chart above shows some typical quantitative programline data for our FCBH programs in Africa for 2009. Notice that the chart is reporting "Proclaimers sent". That is the actual number of Proclaimers physically produced and shipped to our Africa partners from our Albuquerque offices in 2009. Our partners may report that of all the Proclaimers sent each one started a FCBH group; however, we cannot verify that by our baseline data. Otherwise the programline data and the baseline data did mirror each other closer than we expected to see.

For every 100 Proclaimers used to start listening groups...

An Additional 30 groups were formed

292 people gave their lives to Christ

184 people were baptized

14 Churches were planted

76 groups were still active after 7 months

*318 groups were polled in 10 different countries

The chart above shows baseline data collected from 318 groups in West, East, Southern, and Horn of Africa. No one area of Africa was favored in our sample selection. All of these groups were actually visited by our researchers and these are the actual numbers they found on the ground during their visits to the groups. Hosanna had anecdotal reporting of FCBH groups multiplying spontaneously, but this baseline data gives an actual quantitative report on group expansion. On average 30 new additional groups were formed for each 100 Proclaimers used to actually start an FCBH program. The empirical evidence of second generation FCBH groups starting spontaneously was one of our "AHA!" discoveries. Since we now have baseline data to support spontaneous generation of FCBH, it will become a feature of our reporting forms to be used with partners. This spontaneous generation of second (and, we believe, third generation) groups also suggested an first answer to one of our beginning questions: Is FCBH, as an oral strategy, reproducible on the field without inputs of western funding and direction? Obviously, the end users have shown us the way, and in response we are now building reproduction of groups into our initial training of FCBH implementers.

The chart above contained other surprising information. For each 100 FCBH groups actually started using the Proclaimer, 14 new churches were planted. Again, this speaks to the questions of reproducibility and the ability of implementing partners to contextualize FCBH to meet the needs of the people on the receiving end of the ministry. The question naturally arises: "How did Hosanna define 'church planting' for the purposes of this research?" The answer is simple: We did not make any definition of church planting. To do so would be an exercise in ecclesiology, something which Hosanna—as a Bible agency—is not willing to do. Each of our partners has developed their own definition of "church plant" and our field researchers simply reported what they saw applying the definitions of the partner who was implementing FCBH. A long discussion about church planting methodology and meaning could ensue at this point, but it is outside of the expertise and mission of Hosanna to do so. Regardless of the meaning applied by our field partner, the data definitely shows some additional reproducible activity being called "church planting" is happening in addition to the spontaneous generation of listening groups. This was a second "AHA!" moment for us. We knew that in some applications some church planting had occurred; however, to what extent that happened across the entire program was unclear.

Of course the greatest story in the "Africa Average" chart is the number of conversions to Christ reported. Hosanna had initially conceived of Faith Comes By Hearing as a discipleship methodology for oral cultures. We had gone into the field assuming that

FCBH would be primarily a church based program to engage Christians in the scriptures. We had also assumed that additional people would come to faith in Christ as a result of obedience to the Word of God, but evangelism was not our primary target. Making disciples in oral cultures was our primary target. That making disciples in oral cultures is an actual result of FCBH is borne out by the surprising amount of evangelism that happens alongside—or, as a result—of making disciples. This would seem to be a Biblical expectation for in the Book of Acts there are many examples of evangelism resulting from the making of disciples.

Looking At A Typical Program

Not every program was as completely successful as the Africa average. A typical partner in Uganda and one in Tanzania demonstrate the wide variety of results that could be achieved using FCBH as a methodology for discipleship in oral communities. The chart that follows is from our Uganda partner.

UGANDA PARTNER:

For every 100 Proclaimers used to start listening groups...

No additional groups were formed

120 people gave their lives to Christ

120 people were baptized

4 Churches were planted

84 groups were still active after 7 months

*25 groups were polled in Uganda

It is obvious from this chart not every program is successful with spontaneous generation of new groups. In looking closer at the actual programs we found that the FCBH program was initially introduced into the more stable traditional churches in Uganda at first[16]. This would seem to explain the higher stability of the groups (84 groups were still active after 7 months), and the lower number of Churches planted as a result of FCBH activity. Even so, the report of 120 people converted to Christ and 120 people baptized is very encouraging. This is also one of the partnerships where we found the audio scripture recordings were being used by a radio station. The manager of that radio station reported that they had experienced increased listenership during the time the audio scriptures were played. In addition, he reported that listeners came to the radio station with their questions--delivered either orally or in writing. The radio station uses local pastors to answer questions on the air.   This interesting use of FCBH by our field partner in Uganda also raises the question of scalability of FCBH as a program in oral cultures. This is not the first experience we have had with FCBH broadcast by radio, and the results are similar to other radio station uses of audio scriptures for FCBH. What made this particular radio use of interest to us was (a.) the program is done only with the audio scriptures without a typical radio introduction and program closing. And, (b.) the local radio station and pastors had devised their own method of "closing the loop" of communication by encouraging listeners to send their questions to the radio station. Our field researcher noted, "So many people have loved this program because wherever they are, at work, home, etc., they have a chance to participate in the discussion after listening to the Word."[17] The discussion evidently takes place spontaneously where groups of people listen as well by the forwarding of questions to the radio station.

Our Uganda partner represents a rather typical church based FCBH program implemented by a Bible agency. It should be noted that Bible agencies, by definition, are not usually church planting organizations. It should also be noted that our Uganda partner was working primarily with main stream Christian churches, and primarily not with the new religious movements that spring up everywhere in Africa. Even so, there is a sharp contrast between the outcomes of FCBH in Uganda and those of another of our implementing partners working in Tanzania. This partner's evangelism/discipleship strategy is to show the JESUS Film in each village, city, and town in Tanzania. They have mapped the entire country down to the sub-village level and have an organized program for showing the JESUS Film. Each year this partner shows the JESUS Film six to seven thousand times. We were able to partner with them in a discipleship follow-up methodology using FCBH and The Proclaimer. At the time of the post-project verification research they had established about 800 audio scripture listening programs.

TANZANIA PARTNER:

For every 100 Proclaimers used to start listening groups...

An additional 44 groups were formed
484 people gave their lives to Christ
808 people were baptized
36 Churches were planted
76 groups were still active after 7 months
Groups listen to 4 Chapters at a time
Of the active groups, 67% listened 2X a week while the rest listened once a week
*25 groups were polled in Tanzania

This partner, for internal reasons, was unable to give us the kind of reporting normally proscribed by the FCBH program. At the time of the post-project verification research we were seriously considering whether Hosanna should continue to invest valuable resources into this project. As you can see from the chart above, this partner is one of our stellar FCBH programs in Africa. The partner works primarily in rural areas and does few, if any, showings in larger towns or cities at this time. So, the primary recipient of this partner's ministry are both economically disadvantaged and primarily non-literate. The majority of the FCBH audio scripture listening programs we verified with this partner were established in the Maasai speaking areas of Northern Tanzania.

Two items on the Tanzania partner chart caught my interest. The number of new groups established, and churches planted. These numbers speak to reproducibility of the FCBH methodology and demonstrate how the partner contextualized the methodology to fit their particular needs. In the case of the Tanzania partner the number of secondary groups that spontaneously started for each 100 Proclaimers used was 44. This is a sharp contrast with the figure of zero for the Uganda partner. The number of churches planted in Tanzania represents a 900% increase in church planting over the Uganda figure of 4, and a 257% increase in church planting over the Africa average. This is a partner that is clearly making good use of the FCBH methodology for both discipleship and church planting. The number of new converts to Christ reported in the Tanzania random sample represented a 165.7% increase over the Africa average.

What is even more impressive is the qualitative reporting that comes from the field notes. Generally speaking, there is usually a low level of hostility between the Maasai, who are Nilotic cattle keepers, and their Bantu neighbors.   They are often treated very poorly. One respondent said, "When they go near people of other tribes [Bantus] the people shout, 'toka apo wewe maasai!'" ("Away from here you Maasai!") Two things are notable about this respondent. First, it is a woman who is the group leader—and, women are not held in high esteem by the Maasai culture and are not usually thought of as leaders. Even so, the researcher found three men, 20 women, and 15 children attending this group. Second, the group leader expressed joy at being able to hear the scriptures in the Maasai language. Finding that God could speak in their language was seen as a validation of them as persons.

Groups by Gender

What does a typical FCBH group look like in Africa? Based upon experience with other church based programs in Africa one would expect to see a preponderance of women and children. Aili Mari Tripp, Professor of Political Science and Women's Studies at the University of Wisconsin-Madison writes, "Women's organizations often constituted the largest organized sector in many countries [in Africa]."[18] Tripp goes on to mention that in Kenya women were the fastest growing sector of civil society. This same type of gender disparity between women and men is reported in other research as well. Does this hold true of FCBH as well? The chart below shows the breakdown of group attendance as actually recorded by our field researchers.

GROUP COMPOSITION

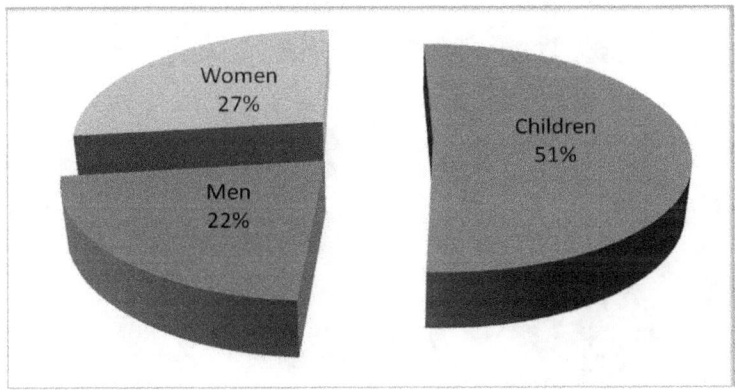

Average # of listeners: 32

From the reports of our field researchers, FCBH presents an unusual demographic for Africa. In FCBH Bible Listening groups there is almost an even number of men and women attending. We expected to see large numbers of women and children in attendance, but the number of men actually seen and counted during site visits is unusual. Does this mean that entire families are listening together? Hopefully the answer is "yes" as suggested by this note from Christine Kituyi on her research in Rwanda, "Families who had drastic problems now have peace. One couple consistently fought but after listening and joining the group 6 months ago are at peace." She goes on to mention that this particular listening group bought zinc roofing sheets to assist one man in the group.[19] This report is not an isolated incident. The field notes from our researchers in every region mention this dynamic.

TYPES OF GROUPS REPORTED

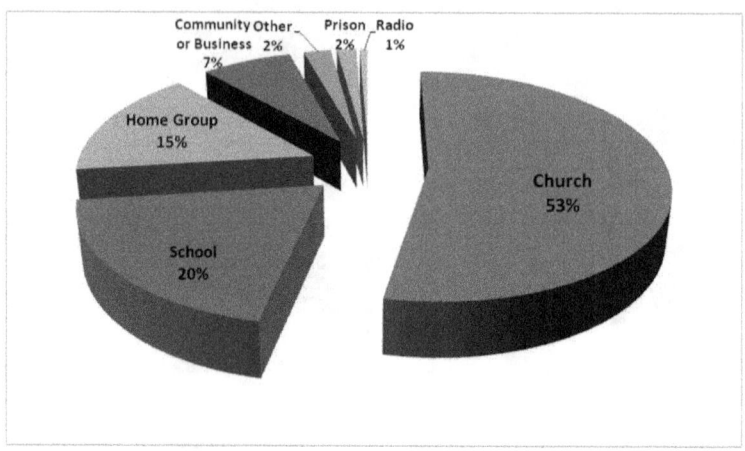

As was discussed in the section entitled "Five Pillars of FCBH" earlier in this study, our initial target was the local church, and our initial FCBH programs were intended to disciple Christians. Our partners on the ground found many other uses for the FCBH audio scripture program which went far beyond our initial target. In the chart above we discovered that while FCBH as a church based program still represents a majority of our listening groups, our partners expanded the methodology far beyond our expectations.

We had received several anecdotal reports of FCBH audio scripture listening being used in prisons in Africa; however, this was our first study to quantify an actual number (which is represented as a percentage in the chart above). Our field partners had immediately seen the value of the captive audience that the prison presents. As well, the prison administrators saw the potential for involving prisoners in a positive activity. As a result we are working more intentionally with our FCBH implementers to expand this kind of ministry opportunity. Our partner in South Africa has recently received government approval for the FCBH program and the Proclaimer to be used in all prison facilities in the country.

Hosanna has an international partnership with Scripture Union (SU) in Africa; however, the SU programs are not reflected in the school statistics of this study. The school programs represented in this research consist of spontaneous school programs started by field partners who saw the need. In most cases when there is a mention of a school program the picture that comes to mind is one of eager primary or secondary school students listening in school classrooms. That is not always the case. One of our school programs included in this study was actually in a vocational school setting, Owusu Dressmaking. "[The] group consist of young girls, most of whom in need of guidance and the Word of God to stand for Jesus." The report goes on to list "transformation in the lives of the apprentices" as one of the positive impacts of audio scripture listening.[20]Our discovery that school-based programs are so well received has prompted us to develop a modified form for our field research tool to use with school based programs. Our newest School Listening Group Report form that our researchers are using tracks additional quantitative data. We hope in the future to be able to give an assessment of the impact of the school based programs based upon better empirical data.

Of special interest is the 7% slice of the chart labeled "Community Other or Business". We were very surprised to discover that in some areas local businesses would either shut down for one hour per week to listen to audio scriptures, or, they played the audio scriptures in their places of business. It is rare in a Western setting for business owners to provide Bible study opportunities for the workers; however, that is not so in Africa. From the field notes of Charles Fumadorh, our West African researcher, are remarks about a listening group at the Stanley Fitting Shop[21] in Ghana. Charles observed, "Other fitters in the vicinity come to join them in the listening." Charles goes on to note "this group is already listening to Revelation 12-13." The make-up of this group, like the dressmakers group mentioned above, is primarily—but not exclusively--apprentices. Some car owners or drivers who frequent the shop make it a point to stop in for listening as well. Charles reports, "Lively debates are generated from the listeners." Lively debate is indicative of serious engagement with the scriptures presented by the audio Bible. Our research also discovered FCBH being used with intentionality with the police. The researcher noted that, "Different officers now are fighting corruption among the rank & file"[22] Another FCBH group located in a business in Uganda noted, "This is very good for the [people working in the market] who may not have time for church [services]"[23]

OF THE GROUPS WE SURVEYED:

83% listen weekly

11% listen twice a week

5% listen daily

1% listen monthly

How consistently do FCBH groups meet? Our intended program (the Five Pillars of FCBH) envisioned groups meeting once a week at a regular time. Since rural African culture tends to prioritize event over time, this is a likely a very western kind of thinking. Our end users—the implementers of FCBH —actually improved upon the program. As you can see from the chart above 99% of the active groups surveyed meet once a week or more, with some meeting daily to listen to the audio scriptures. This is similar to the spontaneous growth of second—and, possibly third—generation groups mentioned above. The end user identifies that having the Proclaimer available for use only one day a week is not a satisfactory use of the resource. Therefore, the program expands to fill the time available rather than restricting access to just one day per week. Only 1% of the groups surveyed listen to the audio scriptures less than the anticipated once a week. This represents 1% of all active FCBH groups which fail to thrive for a variety of reasons.

Understanding the Qualitative Data

Following the Grounded Theory methodology, the collected field notes and narrative reports from the field researchers were read dozens of times by the Africa group based in Albuquerque. It was our hope to view the Faith Comes By Hearing program through the eyes of the end users. This required developing a practice of listening and recording comments and input from the field. We were not interested in simply compiling quantitative statistics—as important as they are to the study. In reading the field notes and narrative reports some common patterns began to emerge from the data. Each of the people reading the reports began to build lists of what they considered to be common patterns of comments. The team would meet regularly to compare notes and challenge the insights of other team members. We tried as much as possible to allow the data to speak for itself, and not impose our grid of expectations on the data. This exercise took approximately two months. At the end of this step we had identified more than 181 patterns of comments that fell into twelve categories of concern.

After identifying each of these patterns and the category under which they belonged we created a coding chart that gave each of the patterns a distinct code number. The field notes and narrative reports were read once again. This time each sentence in the report was read for content and patterns observed in the sentence were coded into the margins of the data. Following that step the individual codes were entered into an excel spreadsheet along with all the quantitative data for each individual group visited. In this way both quantitative and qualitative data for each group visited was kept connected to the group trom which it came. We are still mining this data for additional insights, so what is presented here is a sample of our initial discoveries.

FAMILY IMPACT:

Family noticed change in students/children

Life transformed through hearing Bible

Families live in peace

Families listen together

Families reconciled

Parents asked school teachers about FCBH

Unity

Relationships restored

Marriages healed

Children/students better behaved

One of our initial discoveries concerned family impacts of the Faith Comes By Hearing audio Bible discipleship program. We discovered that the category of "Family Impact" was mentioned 65 times by respondents in the field and our field researchers in their notes. The chart above shows the patterns of comments ranked in the order of frequency of mention. The top three comments were especially revealing. Comparing the first comment, "Family noted change in children/students" with the chart on page 27 shows a consistency between the qualitative data and the quantitative data. The majority of Faith Comes By Hearing participants are children. It would stand to reason that if the FCBH program has impact on the majority of participants it would be noted by parents and other adults.

Respondents also had quite a bit to say about improvement in family relationships. In Tanzania,

Stanley Mindeibu of the Mdoni Mgingo village reports the following about a family in his listening group: "Those who were hearing God [through the Proclaimer] are now changed. The Maasai women have become involved in discussing about God. The listening group is held at [a] man's house who has 3 wives and yet they were fighting a lot. After listening to the Proclaimer they now have peace in the home. He and his wives plus the whole family have been Baptized."[24] This seems to underscore the unusual gender balance of typical FCBH groups, and at the same time demonstrate effectiveness of oral scripture use within family systems in oral cultures— even those systems thought to be foreign to western ideas.

Two things should be made plain in this paper. First, we have yet to complete the task of "mining" our qualitative data. That will take place over the next few months at Hosanna. Secondly, what we want to present here is "photograph" in time of our program. A true photograph will also show the flaws or mistakes happening on the ground with our partners as well as the strengths. We have no intention of puffing the positive data or hiding negative data about FCBH.

In doing our preliminary mining of the data we discovered that barriers to listening were mentioned almost as many times as family impact. It is important for us to understand the barriers that we face in the implementation of FCBH so that creative solutions can be devised to meet these challenges. The chart below shows the barriers to listening to the audio scriptures as seen by the end user of FCBH in the field.

BARRIERS TO LISTENING:

Farming/work

Wrong language used/other(s) needed

Time not convenient

Persecution

Too many other programs

Too busy, no time for group

Travel distances/road conditions

Family/peer pressure

Funeral

War/conflict/theft/safety issues

Of the top three perceived barriers to listening the second most often mentioned barrier surprised us greatly. Since Hosanna/FCB works only with strategic partnerships on the field, we assumed that our partners knew what language to use in the implementation of the FCBH program in their area. That assumption was proven to be a false assumption. The groups mentioning "wrong language" came primarily from large international partnerships[25] where majority language speakers simply assumed that the language of wider communication would be as effective as the specific language of the area. This was a great disappointment to us since the entire purpose of FCBH is to get the New Testament in the heart language into the groups. Even more frustrating to my team at Hosanna was the fact that, in most cases, the proper language was available in recorded format from Hosanna! This discovery has caused our Field Coordinators and USA staff to work more closely with each of our partners to reinforce the understanding of the importance of using the proper local language in the FCBH program. Is this an intrinsic flaw in FCBH? No. We determined that it was a training issue that could be dealt with when training our partners to do FCBH.

The number one barrier to listening, "Farming/work" did not surprise us at all. I have not yet seen qualitative research from other oral discipleship methodologies; however, I would guess that all the methodologies would face this problem at some time. We had known for years that when rainy season comes, the rural people will largely be unable to invest their time in any other activity than farming. This has not created a permanent barrier to FCBH, rather it is a seasonal barrier. Successful listening groups meet this challenge by either increasing the number of times they listen to the audio scriptures per week during the dry season, or, by suspending temporarily the listening program during the farming season. The program is re-established again during the dry season.

Some of the other perceived barriers to listening reflect the comments of urban groups (i.e. "time not convenient", "too many other programs", etc.) It may be that alternative approaches to FCBH such as more individualized programs in urban areas, making the audio scriptures available for wide distribution via web and cell phone not connected to an official program may surmount these barriers. Hosanna has taken the steps of making the audio scriptures available by digital means outside of the traditional FCBH program.[26] This serves to make the audio New Testament "scaleable" to serve any size of group including individuals.

Why Groups Fail

The research clearly demonstrates that not every FCBH group is successful. The chart below shows the top six reasons for FCBH group failures.

WHY GROUPS FAIL:

Equipment performance

Leader not committed

Leader moved

Farming

Not trained

Persecution

Critics of the use of audio scriptures as a discipleship tool in oral cultures will no doubt say, "I told you so!" when seeing the number one cause of group failure. It is true that our initial experience with the Proclaimers in the field revealed some problems with the rechargeable batteries that created unnecessary equipment problems. It is also true that a majority of the groups surveyed in this research were using the older battery technology, thus the high number of mentions in the data. However, any other digital player device using the same battery technology was vulnerable to the same outcomes. So, this problem was not specific to the Proclaimer. Initially, when the problem was discovered, it was referred to the engineering staff of Hosanna for assistance in solving the problem. The engineering staff did make recommendations about conditioning the batteries before releasing the Proclaimers into the field. This battery conditioning process, while highly successful in alleviating problems, was time consuming for some of our partners to follow. In addition to developing a battery conditioning protocol, the Africa team in the USA also developed a protocol for replacement of failed batteries and corrupted flash memories within 48 hours of being notified by our partners of the failures. In some cases, partners delayed notifying us of non-functional Proclaimers. This required us to train our Field Coordinators to visit our implementing partners in their area and look for equipment problems. They were equipped with technical knowledge to, in some cases, resurrect non-functional Proclaimers on the spot. The current model of the Proclaimer now being used in the field has a vastly improved battery and battery charging system. This has reduced equipment failure problems to almost nil.

Some of the other reasons listed for group failure (i.e. "leader not trained", "leader moved", and "leader not committed") we identified as training issues. Our Field Coordinators along with our USA staff have worked to improve our training materials. We are also more closely screening our potential field partners to better assess their capacity for taking on the task of FCBH and their competency in training FCBH workers.

Conclusions

While we are still processing data from our field notes, the initial results definitely show that not only is FCBH a viable long term strategy for discipleship in oral communities, it is also reproducible without inputs of western funds or training. We worked hard to make certain that data in the research came from all four of the main regions of Africa: West Africa,

164

East Africa, Horn of Africa, and Southern Africa. We did not want to have a regional bias in our results. We were not afraid to show clearly some of the negative data. We wanted the research to address fairly both the positive impact and the challenges facing the FCBH program. After review this research some areas of concern were addressed, and we believe that subsequent field research will demonstrate that these challenges have been surmounted. This research took a brutally honest look at our own program, and found factual evidence to support our contention that audio scriptures are a valuable tool for use in making disciples in oral cultures.

Is FCBH the *only* methodology appropriate for discipleship in oral communities? No. The research does not bear out that conclusion; however, where a New Testament in the target language already exists it may be the most effective methodology. There is room for many other methodologies to be developed for making disciples in oral settings. Especially in those cultures where there is no New Testament available in the target language. In those cases Hosanna is proactively seeking to engage partners with other methodologies, hoping to share what we have learned as well as bring to the partnership some valuable skills.

From this initial research Hosanna/FCBH is now expanding "Rice Checking" into other regions served by the ministry. In 2011 the Latin America region will be conducting the same exercise. We will fold those results into our established data base. I believe we will find similar results in that region.

Submitted by Greg Fisher, Faith Comes by Hearing
GFisher@FCBHmail.org

Section Three:
Internet/Mobile

Internet/Mobile Case 1: The Prophets' Story

Category: Social Media/Cell Phone
Location: Asia

The Prophets' Story *video is an animated gospel presentation that can be quickly translated into new languages. We tried to make an "open" video, similar to "open source" software, which anyone could translate, use and in the process create a tool for others ministering to that language group to use, crowd-sourcing the translations.*

Strategic Objective

Provide a digital culture with a digital gospel track that could be easily adapted to new language groups.

·Create a complete and concise animated gospel presentation based on proven gospel sharing methods from the Middle East and Asia.
·Create a website where different language versions

of the video can be downloaded for the user's specific device
·Create an instructional video and an easy process that will help facilitate the most translations possible
·Promote translating the video in missionary circles, missions events and college campus ministries with high populations of internationals.
·Optimize the website per language group, targeting keywords in these minor languages that are still highly searched but with low competition.
·Work with Translation Facilitators to develop an online follow-up system.

Area of its Use (target group)

·Primarily Asia but really anywhere a motivated facilitator emerges. So far it has been used in various parts of Indonesia, Bangladesh, India, South Lebanon, China and Hong Kong, and several college campuses around the US.

Estimated Audience

·YouTube, Google searches, FB ads and friend links

How was it produced?

·Local Christian workers saw the need for having a digital track for short term teams to sow the gospel broadly if no translator was available.
·Together with a media team in SE Asia, we scripted, animated and scored the video presentation.

Which organizations were involved in the process?

·Antioch Community Church and their partners in SE Asia.

Research

·The presentation itself is an adaptation of a method of
sharing the gospel which proved successful in the
Middle East. As cross cultural workers adopted the
method, they saw an increase in understanding and
effectiveness. Another contributing factor to its
success, however, was a strategy shift from more
focused sowing of the gospel to a much broader
sowing.
·Short term mission trips in various countries field tested the
video. Translations of the film were preloaded on
team members' smart phones and media players
before they came which gave them familiarity with
the presentation and keywords in the local
language. They shared in malls, city squares and
homes with people who showed interest in the
gospel. Those who remained interested after
hearing the full gospel presentation were then
referred to nationals who could better answer their
specific questions and assist them further.

Current status? Where is it used?

·<u>Finished</u> - Create a complete and concise animated gospel
presentation based on proven gospel sharing
methods from the Middle East and Asia.
·<u>In Process</u> - Create a website where different language
versions of the video can be downloaded for the
user's specific device
·<u>In Process</u> - Create an instructional video and an easy
process that will help facilitate the most translations
possible

·<u>In Process</u> - Promote translating the video in missionary circles, missions events and college campus ministries with high populations of internationals.

·<u>Not yet started</u> - Optimize the website per language group, targeting keywords in these minor languages that are still highly searched but with low competition.

·<u>In-Process</u> - Work with Translation Facilitators to develop an online follow-up system.

<u>http://theprophetsstory.com</u>

FMI: <u>theprophetsstory@gmail.com</u>

Internet/Mobile Case 2: Web-Comic

Category: Web-Comic
Location: China

Little Fish in a Big Pond *is a daily web-comic that follows the lives of Ma Ya Nan and Wang Xiao Yu, two freshman university students in China.*

Synopsis: Through the daily adventures of Ma Ya Nan, Xiao Yu, and their classmates, we experience the challenges, triumphs, heartaches and joys of university life. It is in English at www.littlefishcomic.com and Mandarin at www.xiaoyudachi.com with links in between. Critical faith issues are brought up and the characters experience the pressures common to Chinese university students and there is an online forum.

Strategic Objective

1) To help 17-25 year old university students cope with the pressures of life in China.

2) To help Chinese university students understand, through identification with the characters, critical faith issues and get them talking about them on newly rolled out forums. The goal of the story is to deal with issues common to young people in China and to show redemptive answers and value positive responses to some of those common issues. We also see the characters in the story interact with gospel elements (forgiveness, mercy, grace, hope, justice, and

punishment for wrongdoing), and some characters eventually come to faith in direct ways, although this is drawn out over the course of the story.

Countries and Region of its Use

LF has regular visitors from China, Taiwan, Hong Kong, Singapore, Malaysia and the USA.

Estimated Audience

To date we have seen over 35,000 visit the English site and 27,000 visit the Mandarin site from well over 15 countries worldwide. Of those 1,109 are unique visitors to the Mandarin site and 1,715 are unique to the English site.

Promotion

Initially, the writer made a presentation to the English Language Institute of China orientation session in early October 2010 and passed out free posters for teachers to put into their classrooms. Mission personnel were also informed and a number asked for posters. The sites were networked among others who target Chinese people.

Initial Site Promotion

Dates	Mandarin	English
Oct 1-December 11th	Less than 4500 visits	Less than 5000 visits
January 12, 2011	8,787	11,044
April 15, 2011	24,328	35,835

There were also about 100 individuals who joined the online forum. Due to a computer glitch these "members" were lost but we are developing a new forum strategy that will "save" information off server.

Clustr Maps: On December 11, 2010 we implemented a web system that started to track unique URL locations. A separate map was put on the two separate sites. While we could see the regular hit counter rising, we could now track where they were coming from. With this we started to see that the majority of the unique visitors were coming from the USA, Taiwan and mainland China. Regular hit counts went up sharply also. This varied from the Mandarin site to the English one.

Facebook: On December 20, 2010 a Facebook ad campaign was started. While it is true that FB is blocked by the PRC, there are still 99,000 Chinese mainland users who most likely visit through a VPN. However, there are 7,485,000 in Taiwan, 3.5 million in Hong Kong, 2.1 million in Singapore as well as the diaspora who are FB users. Starting with the ad on the left, we varied the ads and targets. When a user clicks on the ad in FB, it goes to (in this case) the English version of the site. This ad, targeting Hong Kong and China has had 1.2 million page views and stimulated over 200 site visits. The most interesting ad is English, targeting Singaporeans and Malaysians who list Chinese on their FB profile. In the first 2 days, there were 91,000 views and 55 click-throughs.

Facebook Character Pages: On Dec 27, 2010 we established FB identities for the two main characters, Ya Nan (main female) and Xiao Yu (main male). Starting a manual "friend acquisition" technique by sending out invitations to Chinese-name individuals, Ya

Nan has 88 FB friends and Xiao Yu 33. We also have a Little Fish Comic FB Group with 8 members. There is also a FB badge on the comic sites to drive traffic to FB from the site.

Rank Page: One February 1, 2011 we entered into an SEO service and optimized the site for the term "Online Chinese Comics" and raised the search rank on Google, Bing and Yahoo from well over 100 to less than 5 on each of the sites. This cost $250 and we deactivated the service after a month, leaving the ranking improved.

Cards: In the next few months we will include a promotion card in packets of Christian materials given to mainland Chinese tourists in Hong Kong, Taiwan and Thailand.

Promotion Conclusions

It is clear that in this case the majority of the visitors came from the Facebook promotion. It has been difficult to get company personnel involved to date however we do believe if we can give cards to hand out this will increase direct interaction.

We would also like to print the comics in-country and will work on an Amazon Print on Demand version which should appeal to the non-mainland market.

How was it produced?

A media use questionnaire was sent out to various personnel in Greater China. One worker had mentioned his interest in a comic project, just to paste broadsheets on signboards on the university campus. He was in Bangkok for the birth of their 2nd child and was heading out on leave (and as it turned out, an extended medical leave). An entire year passed with us emailing ideas back and forth and in March 2010 we visited his family. We ironed out the storyline and he started writing.

At the same time we started looking for Chinese comic artists who would be willing to handle the 5 pages per week we needed for this project. I approached the Rox35's Nathan Butler and other Chinese GCCs. Although a number of artists were approached none were willing. We decided to outsource both sketching and ink and color to another country using a GCC media outsourcing partner. We launched in October 2010 as a web comic.

Conclusion

•We rolled out the two sites on October 6th. To date we have seen over 35,000 visit the English site and 24,000 visit the Mandarin site from well over 15 countries worldwide.

•Promotion on Facebook has increased our unique visitors from Taiwan and Malaysia significantly.

•The development of guides to use the site in teaching English through a "talking/teaching points" curriculum will stimulate English teachers to use the site more effectively.

•We will be developing strategies to get the audience involved in discussing life issues in newly rolled out online forums. On the forum and through some of the user interaction we have gotten feedback that the audience recognizes the story as being about young people in China going to college and accepts it as being true to life and their experiences.

FMI:Dan Henrich - info@comresources.org

Internet/Mobile Case 3: Media Follow-up Systems

Category: Technology
Location: Anywhere

Out of 5.2 billion cell phone subscribers, 4.1 billion are active SMS users.

97% have at least a basic browser (including WAP, not necessarily color)
95% have a color screen - this is 4 Billion, more than twice the number of TV sets and 3x number of PCs
92% are data-capable (at least 2.5G ie GPRS or basic CDMA 2000)
85% support MMS - this is 3.6 Billion, more than twice number of TV sets and 2x active users of eMail
81% are cameraphones - this is 3.4 Billion cameras
76% have a full browser, i.e. HTML type of browser (compare with 17% which is total number of smartphones)
62% have a media player
61% support apps using Java or Brew (compare with 17% which is total number of smartphones)
51% have a memory card slot
35% are 3G phones (not nearly all are on 3G networks)
21% support WiFi
17% are smartphones
12% are second-hand phones (mostly in emerging world countries, but also with younger kids)

Strategy

It is essential that we understand our audience and its media usage as we consider ways to invite feedback from media campaigns. Although broad sowing is a good thing, it would be better to find ways to allow the viewer to ask more questions or ask for the premium (Bible, DVD, etc.) For a number of years, ministries in a major Muslim country have used a Post Office box for responses.

If we were to take advantage of these stats we would prioritize our approaches to a system that handles SMS and then MMS. The goal would be to provide a way for people to respond to the media message, the follow-up missionary to build relationships, lead them to Christ and help them.

Broad sowing efforts like TV programs and literature distribution are to be carried out. How will you propose to manage the follow-up? You know this is needed as there must be a channel for the individual to learn more information.

1) The distributed materials include a stamp or sticker that says: "For a free gift, text this number . . . ."

2) They text the number and are given a "coupon code" and url to download a free ringtone or something similar.

3) At the web page where they go to download their free ringtone, there is an offer to send a free book to them. They complete their name and address, etc. and the book is mailed.

4) At a specified time after the book is sent, the system texts back to them giving them an offer for another free gift if they can answer questions from the book sent to them.

Implementation

The question is how to manage the flow of SMS's and emails. Although there are a variety of commercial packages for this, two have been developed by non-profit groups. Which one you choose depends on the volume and location of your respondees.

Scenario 1: Smaller Outreaches

You are setting up a feedback system that will use one computer, located in the country where the number is, for example, in Latin America or East Africa. FrontlineSMS (http://www.frontlinesms.com) is a free package that has Mac, Windows and Linux versions. They have tested a number of GSM modems and give that information to you. You could use a GSM phone but they are harder to set up. When you download it and set up the system you see a screen that looks vaguely like an Outlook screen with Contact, Messages, Emails and Keyword tabs.

The key here is that FrontlineSMS can only be used when there is exactly one helper and one number. For example, we are coordinating a TV outreach in a Muslim nation where the *Ancient Journeys* series will be shown on six local TV stations. Because they are local, we can customize the SMS and email to that area. The SMS's will be handled by a key national in each area.

Scenario 2: Large campaigns in restricted countries

This involves the implementation of a software package called the Relationship Development System or RDS.

RDS is a larger scale system that can handle multiple follow-up personnel in multiple countries.

The RDS includes a Server that connects to the media in three ways:

1. SMS in restricted access areas - In this application the server connects to small computers with regular GSM type modems in-country called "Gateways". The Gateway manages the flow of SMS messages from responders through a secure internet connection to the Server.

2. Email in any situation - an email address is published and that email is directed through the server to the RDS client. RDS manages the flow of emails and respondents can be assigned to specific helpers.

How both systems work:

The Volunteer Helper logs onto the RDS system whereever they live and Frontline(FL) locally to build relationships with contacts. The systems allow users to view and store any kind of correspondence received from a contact, including their contact details or specific details on their spiritual progress. Typically, content from responses are used for programs, and users reply to specific questions and comments from contacts in an endeavor to build relationships with them.

Applications

GENERAL LITERATURE/MEDIA FOLLOW-UP - Currently mission personnel who live in more open areas provide tracts or DVDs to local partners to hand out. In some cases there is no follow-up loop at all, or it is dependent on the person to write their cell # on the media. A number or email address can be provided to these local personnel for this purpose. In this case FL could be set up.

BROAD SOWING USING VOLUNTEERS:

Each year, thousands of bags of literature are passed out, for example, to Chinese tourists in Pattaya and Macau. To date, it has been difficult to gauge how effective the outreach has been. Anecdotal data seems to point to very positive responses, but there is little hard data to support individuals being saved and/or becoming a part of a worshipping group.

In this case, RDS is being implemented with Gateways in-country, a server in Germany and helpers trained in Taiwan and Hong Kong.

WEB-SITE FOLLOW-UP

A major ministry in Europe is handling comments and questions from several websites using RDS's ability to connect using an API address.

CELL PHONE Discipleship

Using audio materials already in the hands of itinerant workers in the Middle East, simple mutiple choice questions can be answered using texting.

Pros and Cons

FrontlineSMS
PRO - cheap to implement (under $1,000), easy to use.

CON - for limited use, one computer, one number, one online helper

Relationship Development System
PRO - Many helpers, living anywhere. API Capability. Best for large projects.

CON - difficult to implement and set up. Expensive (Up to $15,000 with 4 numbers in restricted country, leased server and IT consultant plus travel and monthly maintenance)

To Implement FrontlineSMS visit
http://www.frontlinesms.com

If you are considering RDS, contact Dan Henrich - info@comresources.org

Section Four:
Appendices

Appendix One:
A Simple Guide to Media Research

By Dan Henrich

Introduction

The purpose of this section is to introduce to the reader the methods and practice of Focus Group research for visual media. Although there is cross-over to other forms of media, like radio, the author believes that TV and film producers have ignored, for the most part, proper research which would make present and future productions more effective. We will only deal with research as it relates to the reality of the 2/3 World. The booklet is meant as an easy-to-use manual for designing and implementing focus groups overseas.

Throughout the section, I will use several terms which I see as interchangeable. The first is the use of film and video (or for that matter radio, web, event print can be inserted). The second is referring to a media practitioner as 'he'. I do not do this because I think the role can only be filled by the male gender. This is not true and there are many talented women writers, directors, producers, cameramen/persons(!). Indeed, as Christians interested in reaching the lost through media, we seek out, train and encourage women team members!

A third set of terms used interchangeably is "one-third world" and "two-thirds world." "2/3rds World" always refers to the area outside of the so-called 'west', therefore excluding the USA, Canada, Great Britain, western Europe and the seven tiger nations. This is evolving as mass media becomes social media and news agencies are replaced by citizen journalists.

We will describe approaches and methodology of research that are best used in areas where the extended family is still an vital part of life, where marriages are often arranged and the superstitions of animistic religions still 'stunt' the growth of the Gospel.

Why Visual Media Research?

Research into why a specific television show or film is effective is one of the most important things we can do as producers. The reason is simple. TV is impacting the 2/3rds world now and in the next 10 years even access to TV will explode. It must be a significant part of our 'media-mix' and it must be used effectively. Just as the Children of Israel sent spies into the land which God promised them, we need to use research to know the "lay of the land."

Motivation for Research

Researchers have differing motivations for conducting research. The prime reason is to find out what the audience (or potential audience) is interested in seeing, what they feel strongly about. Many times, the motivations revolve around fundraising. Certainly with Focus Group methodology you will not get any sort of audience count. For instance, if the only reason you conduct postproduction research is to find out what percentage of the viewers 'prayed the sinners prayer', then at the very least a more quantitative approach is necessary. If you wish to find out what sort of response you might receive if you transmitted the program on the national network, then focus groups are the best bet. The

Focus Group will give you insight to what the audience might feel/believe from your program. While it is true that if your intention is to get people to see their need of a Savior, you will gain insight from the F/G. If you have not included a feedback loop in the TV program (See Case Study 6 - Media Follow-up) then you will not learn if those people were touched by your message. (See Case 11 Indonesia Television for a discussion on this).

Types of Research Methodology

This guide will discuss a method of research called Focus Groups, part of a type of research called Qualitative Analysis. The three types of research formats that fall into qualitative analysis are:

In-depth Interviews

This is like the name. The interviewer sits down with his interviewee and they talk for a period of time. Through interview techniques, the interviewer asks a number of questions that allow him to collect pertinent data. This is also called 'key informant' interviewing. It is the lowest stress to the interviewee.

Focus Groups

Focus Group (F/G) research was made popular by the advertising industry. The agencies would gather together groups of 'consumers' and test a product, a commercial, etc. F/G can be used to gain insight into peoples attitudes. Questions are asked in an open ended manner, and the interviewer may get an answer he did not expect. The look on his face and his response will determine whether the interviewee's next response is as honest.

F/G are used to allow the participants to discuss a topic among themselves with the interviewer stimulating the process. The premise is that free discussions generate fresh ideas and insights.

Community Interviews

Unlike F/Gs, in community interviews the 'investigator' asks questions, raises issues, and seeks responses from the participants. The primary interaction is between the investigator and the participants, not between the participants themselves.

Many times, we as producers have a strong desire to make a film. We think that we have a message. Yes, we do have a message, that of salvation. But we need to understand how Jesus can affect the lives of our target audience. We have to listen!

Quantitative Research

This method of research will have a different type of result. It is a list of questions carefully developed by the researcher with a yes/no response or a scaled response, e.g., "The video you just viewed discussed the issue of barrenness. On a scale of 1-10 ..."

What you discover in quantitative research methodology are issues related to demographics, i. e., how a certain age group or sex felt about your film. The problem is that you can lead an interviewee in his or her response to your question because they may be more inclined to tell you what you wish to hear.

When do I conduct research?

There are three stages of the production process where research should take place. These are: pre-production, pre-release and post-release research to improve your communication.

Pre-Production Research
We do not have all the answers. Pre-production research is probably one of the most important parts of *any* media effort.

Some years ago, the author embarked with a team on a project to produce a series of dramatic programs to help Africans understand Christianity in the light of the cultural pressures they faced.

A focus group was gathered of media practitioners and pastors. The result was 52 key issues they believed affected their lives! The type of film we made was heavily influenced by that group -- and it was not what we had planned to do! But we did what the national believers told us to do.

What we found from this focus group was the nature of the topic and the format of the film. It was up to the writing team, two Africans and one American (the author), to develop the characters and scenario, which was again discussed with the same focus group and modified. Then the final script was written and again tested both with the focus group and with a panel of independent readers in several African countries! (See Case 1 - Dramatic Film Africa for a discussion of this film, *Sabina's Encounter*)

Pre-Release Research
In modern Hollywood filmmaking, the industry tests several endings of a film to see which one is liked by the viewers. A misjudgment in this area can mean millions in lost revenue!

Depending on the results, a film can be re-edited prior to release. It is well worth the effort to gather together a focus group to see a DVD 'cut' prior to final confirmation.

With a wise facilitator the producer can learn a lot about how his final film will be received and how the audience will interpret his film interpretations of the script. He might be 'right on' or way off.

Post Release Research
Usually, this stage of research comes after the film has been in circulation for a period of time. It is certainly essential in the event that the producer is making a series. It is essential to know if the film is reaching the audience with the message you wished to communicate in the first place. It is also helpful to know how your characters impacted the viewers. Issues like these should be researched: Was the setting realistic? How was the costuming? What was the perceived theme?

A Philosophy to Research in the 2/3rds World

Part & parcel to any development of a personal philosophy regarding involvement in the research process is an understanding of the role of the western mission worker. Much has been done on the so-called mission fields of Africa and Asia without any research into what the so-called 'target audience' wants!

Strategies are developed in isolation of the group who is supposed to benefit from the program, and the result has not been positive to the long-term growth of the church overseas. A retired American executive once told a story about how he came to Kenya to dig wells in rural villages. Of course, it is a well known fact that clean water should be one of the priorities anywhere, second only to latrines. The man went to the chief and elders and talked about wells and how important they were. But finally after he finished his sales pitch and they were eating together, the man noticed that the elders weren't so happy with the well. So he asked, what was it that they wanted. The answer?

A soccer field!

The retired executive was shocked. It seemed that the elders and the Chief felt that if they had a soccer field and some balls, the village would have a place where they could have some recreation together. They would feel good about themselves and then they would dig their own well!

The executive listened to all this and decided that this was certainly far out of line with the aims of his mission agency but he would take a risk. He assisted them in the grading of the field and bought some balls and went off to his next set of villages. A few weeks later he came back and found that the field had indeed done what the chief and elders had predicted. The men and women had dug a well themselves!

They 'owned' the well and it was being used by the women to draw water instead of the stream! The lesson learned here is that the 'target group' or 'stakeholder' participated in the process of this rural development project. Through the process of consensus through dialogue and risk taking by the retired executive, the project succeeded.

In research, we must take on some of the same aspects of the executive in the example above. The researcher must be willing to take a back seat in the development of question formats. He must depend heavily on his local counterpart from the target region or country.

The researcher must ask him/herself:

What information is needed and what will it be used for? Usually, we determine that we need research to prove a specific point.

Can we use existing research? Maybe, maybe not. Recently a research 'statistic' was discussed at a meeting of media executives that a secular research group had found that more that 70% of the people in the capital city of a certain poor 3rd World nation had TV sets. So, if a program is aired on all the TV stations this agency could reach over three million people with a message of salvation. This group continued to say that they could apply the statistic to the other large cities in this country and reach 70% of the country for Christ.

Then, based on a study in an entirely different region and one campaign they estimated that one in six would accept Christ! So, because of the overall urbanization rate in the country, this group of well-meaning people extrapolated that over three million would accept Christ from one series of broadcasts! In this case, statistics were used to validate fundraising programs!

In other cases research may be used to validate a certain programming approach. There are many cases of both the former and the latter in the missionary media ministries today. These are negative uses of information because they do not take into consideration the stakeholder in the process!

How will I get this information and what questions will I ask? As foreign researchers, we very early in the process find a local counterpart facilitator in our target culture. This counterpart will become a co-researcher in the process. He or she will be essential to bridging the cultural distance between you and the 'stakeholders' in the project. Certainly, you are at risk personally in the research process. But the national facilitator and the stakeholders are equally at risk - a fact that we foreigners ignore or downplay in our own minds.

With this guide, sit down with your counterpart facilitators and discuss what type of information you wish to know from the focus groups. Share with him what you are planning to do with the information, and that he or she will have access to a final report of the findings.

Taking the principles found in this guide, talk through with your counterpart how you wish the F/G approached and what question format is most effective among his people. It may be that he or she feels a certain questioning route is best. In Africa, most certainly the cultural pattern of starting with the general and moving to the specific should be followed.

How will I ask these questions? How will I ask these questions without committing cultural mistakes that would affect my data? By listening to your counterpart researcher. He or she will not want to commit cultural errors and indeed it will be more difficult for them to do so.

The Role Redefined

As foreign researchers, we must take the role of enabler, of trainer, of listener in the process of research design and implementation. This paradigm shift is as essential in research as it has been in the modern missions movement. Nationals must own the projects we wish to implement just as the village mentioned earlier owned the well because they participated in the process of decision making and implementation. We must ensure that the national church 'owns' the research project we want to undertake and especially the media project we intend to produce with the research! As such, the roles:

Enabler

This relates to our position in the decision making process. We must listen, comprehend the answers and be willing to do what the counterpart says. And if that means financing a soccer field instead of a well, so be it! To enable means to "provide with a means or opportunity, to make possible or to sanction." This is opposite of a dictatorial, *I know what is right for you* approach. As an enabler, we are partners in the process of mission and research!

Trainer

The counterpart researcher may not have training in conducting a F/G. So your role becomes a trainer, a person who takes enough time to ensure that the person has an understanding of the process. You transfer the ability to facilitate the F/G to the counterpart. This is part of a process of skill transference that is so essential to modern missions.

Listener

Part of all of this is your role as a listener. Make sure your counterpart understands that the results of the research will make a difference in the project, that you want to know the heart of his people!

Moderator Roles

Beginning the F/G discussion
Beginnings are essential to breaking the ice in any meeting of people who don't know each other. As you know from personal experience, it is essential not to put people off when you first meet.

In the section **Problems of conducting Focus Groups in the 3rd World (see below)** we have discussed problems arising from dress, gender and other specifics. However, it is essential that the moderator create a thoughtful, permissive atmosphere, providing the ground rules and set the tone of the discussion.

Much of the success or failure of the discussion can be attributed to this first 2-3 minutes. For example, too much formality can stifle your discussion, especially the interaction between the participants. Too much informality and humor can cause the participants not to take the discussion seriously.

Moderators with experience in many group situations will tell you that groups are unpredictable: one group will be exciting and dynamic and the next might be restrained and cautious. These differences can be expected. However, the moderator must approach each group in the research project series basically the same way.

It is suggested that the same basic pattern for introducing each group discussion should include:

The Welcome
Overview of topic
Ground rules
First question.

For example, "Good evening and welcome to this discussion tonight. Thanks for taking time to watch the film, and enjoy some snacks with us afterward while we talk about how you feel about the film. My name is _____ from (province) and we are interested in how Kenyans like the translation of *The Hiding Place* in Swahili. The purpose of what we learn from this and other groups will be to help us know how we can create films and videos that you enjoy watching. You were invited tonight because we feel that you are the type of people who will speak their minds in the discussion we will share together afterwards.

This study is being sponsored by _____ here in Nairobi. We would like to ask you back together in a couple of months to review the information we collected from all sorts of people. We want to know that we are reporting the gist of what you feel about the film. So, in the event you want to return for a short meeting to hear about the results and enjoy a meal together, my colleague will pass out a card with a couple of questions on it after the meeting tonight.

I would like to emphasis that there are no right or wrong answers here. Your comments are important. In order to help the discussion along, we have these name tags. Please write the name you feel most comfortable with on these labels.

We will start the film now. It is two hours long. If at any time you wish to use the toilet, it is (place). There are sodas and cakes on the table. My colleague, (name) will assist you."

Show the film - place the food out right at the end.

"Now, please feel free to get some food and as we do," (Ask first question).

Keys to successful 'moderation'

<u>Anticipate the flow of discussion</u>
Since any group discussion is unpredictable, it is important to think through what you are trying to learn about a specific film and consider where that discussion might lead. This will prepare you for such deviations. For example, a focus group

about a film might lead to a series of questions about how the film was made, or the lifestyle of a certain actor if it was locally produced. If this happens, you might want to be ready to counteract that tangent by counteracting with a statement like, "You must remember that we are seeing (actors name) playing a role. So, although we know his lifestyle is not as good as it should be, for the purpose of this discussion it is not important. " A statement of this type should bring the discussion back on track.

Allow differing points of view
You may have said that this is important, but people are not speaking out. Sometimes you just sense by body language that a participant has something different to say, but is restrained by something.

Encourage them again!

Essential techniques
In any conversation a person needs to be concerned with how much one talks. It is easy to dominate the conversation and most novice moderators commit this sin.

Five second pause. This is most often used after a participant comment. It can prompt additional points of views or agreement with the previous point. If also forces you as a moderator from not changing the topic too quickly. Practice it on friends and family to see how effective it can be.

The Probe. This is a request for additional information when people make vague comments with multiple meanings like 'I agree.'
Example of probe questions are:

'Would you explain further'?',
'Would you give us an example of what you mean?'

'Is there anything else?'
'Please describe what you mean?'
'I don't understand.'

It may be important to use the probe early in the discussion to communicate the need for more precision in responses.

Responding to Participant Statements
It is essential that the moderator clearly respond to statements by participants. Sometimes response mechanisms are unconscious.

Head Nodding. One unconscious response is the head nod. This can be helpful if used sparingly and consciously, such as eliciting additional comments from a participant who wishes to talk. But the head nod also signals agreement in some cultures. As such, a head nod signaling agreement may elicit additional comments of the same type, sometimes reinforcing a certain perspective and stifling opposite point of views.

Short Verbal Responses. Depending on our culture, we may have been conditioned to provide short verbal statements to signal acceptance or in some cases simply acknowledge that we heard a statement. Most are acceptable in a focus group setting, e.g., *'OK,' 'yes,' or 'Uh-huh'.* These are value neutral expressions. Responses to avoid are ones which indicate accuracy or agreement. These include, *'correct,' 'that's good,' or 'excellent.'*

Types of Participants
Focus groups bring together a wide variety of personality types. Sometimes specific types of personalities create problems for the moderator. For example:

The Expert. This type of person can inhibit free discussion within a group. They may have considerable experience with the subject under discussion, may have political/social 'clout,' may be an elder in the community or an opinion leader. If you have this type of person in your group, underscore in the introductory comments that all opinions are important.

Dominant Talkers. Often it is this person who thinks they are knowledgeable on the subject but simply have opinions. You can seat this type of person next to you and may be able to exert some level of control by body language or nonverbal clues. Examples of this might be avoiding eye contact with the dominant talker and appearing bored with their statement. In some cases, you may have to simply say, *'Thank you for that comment, does anyone feel differently?*

Shy Respondents. Since they seem to have much to say, but are unwilling to say it due to shyness, attempt to place them directly across from you and maximize eye contact which can encourage them to speak up. If all else fails, ask a direct question.

Rambling Respondents. This type of person drones on and on and rarely gets to the point. Discontinuing eye contact with the 'rambler' after 20-30 seconds can help. Look at your papers, at other participants, look bored, at your watch, etc. As soon as the 'rambler' stops or takes a breath, be ready to fire off another question to divert them. In the remaining discussion avoid making eye contact with them to reduce the potential of another 'ramble.'

Problems of conducting Focus Groups in the 3rd World

The major problems with conducting focus groups in the 2/3rd world revolve around:

Government Approval

In most developing countries, individual freedoms are greatly restricted. In Kenya, you are supposed to get a permit to meet with more than 10 others unless it is an established community or church group. This is ignored in many cases, but can be used as an excuse to close you down if your motivation for being together appears to threaten those in power.

Many times this can be gotten around by getting approval of the local authority, in the case of the Kenyan setting, the chief. The chief is an appointed position and very powerful. Researchers should use a community leader. In any case, although you can mitigate the problems, a reason can always be 'created' by someone to stop you from conducting research.

For example, in the mid-80s, the government sponsored a family planning TV soap opera in Kenya called *Tushariani*. It was very popular and followed some of formats developed by the Indian soap, *Hum Log*. When *Tushariani* was on television, a very large percentage of Kenya was watching it. Unfortunately, it was the special project of the vice-president and when he fell from grace, so did the program.

A researcher interested in producing TV shows and films would find it very worthwhile to see why the show was so popular. However, official support would most likely have been denied until after the VP died. And even so, a thorough analysis of *Tushariani* itself would most likely have to be done at an informal level anyway due to the power structure.

Interpersonal distance between interviewer and focus group(F/G) - This can manifest itself in various ways, e.g.,

Attitude of superiority - The interviewer thinks he is better than the F/G.

Attitude of inferiority - The F/G is older, richer, wiser than the interviewer. For example, using a student to conduct the interview could be offensive to the members.

Language - The interviewer uses terms unfamiliar to the F/G. This could be scientific language or slang; or if the F/G consists of slum youth, the non-use of slang!

Dress - Essential that the interviewer dress like the F/G. Not "up" or "down"!

Tribe - It is important that you appreciate tribal issues. For instance, don't sent a Hutu to interview a Tutsi!

Unplanned Bias

One of the problems of conducting F/Gs is the issue of the introduction of bias. Bias can be introduced in a number of ways:

Interviewer Bias

It is essential that the interviewer be unbiased at all times. Bias can be introduced by the interviewer's unconscious response to something a F/G member might say.

> **Example**: For instance, suppose you are sampling a group of young women on birth control attitudes. Your interviewer is a matron who has a deep-set judgmental attitude toward young women who have sex early. The attitude could seep into how the F/G was conducted and the young women would be less open.

Solution: Thoroughly interview your interviewer. In the example given above, you might uncover her attitudes, and with that understanding you might make sure that the interviewer guards against letting her beliefs affect the F/G. Or, you may decide to get another interviewer!

Designer Bias

It is always problematic when the designer (or researcher) has something he/she wants to prove. Research is rarely done in a vacuum! The designer/researcher can interject bias in the way he/she constructs the questions.

Analysis Bias

Certainly, this is a significant level where bias can be interjected, especially of the results of the F/Gs do not match up with what the researcher wanted to learn.

Environment Issues

There are all sorts of inter-related issues concerning the environment. The goal is to select a place to conduct the F/G where the participants are comfortable and somewhat secluded.

For instance, you might want to avoid a church for a group of slum dwellers who might sleep with whores. Use a location where they might come, such as a community center or something similar. Don't overdue the noise seclusion issue if the participants are used to a noisy environment. For instance, if you wish to talk about parenting methods, it might be better to have a location where the kids are allowed to run free (you might learn more by observation in this case!).

Sample selection

You must have some sort of representative sample whom you are researching. Here are several options:

Census - Choose by general population percentages: Take the known formal or informal census statistics and make sure your group consists of roughly the same.

By target group - If your research is related to a specific demographic group, use a representative sample, e.g., if women, have 100% women, split up into the age demographics. In Kenya, 50 - 55% of the population are women. 80% of the population are under the age of 27. More interestingly, 50% of the total population are under the age of 15!

Discussion Questions

What would be your procedures in selecting a research assistant?

How would you select the participants of a F/G dealing with birth control and virginity? Statistics show that a large percentage of girls in Kenya have their first sexual experience prior to 14 years in age.

Describe the process of developing a series of questions and your role.

Is there a project that you have completed, are working on, or are thinking about or planning that would gain something by a series of Focus Groups?

Appendix Two:
Sample Media Use
Questionnaire

PURPOSE STATEMENT
PLEASE RENAME THIS DOCUMENT WITH YOUR LAST NAME AND SEND IT TO (Email). We would appreciate it if you would complete and return it as soon as possible.

Your Name:	
Your email:	
Where do you live?	
Your Focus Group:	

Check Here	1.) What Media have you used with your target group?
	DVD/ VCD
	TV
	Radio
	Internet
	Cell Phone (SMS/texting)
	Comic Books
	Books
	Magazines
	Tracts

	2.) Please list the media product titles you have used (use as many lines as necessary)
Check & Comment	
	For evangelism
	For basic discipleship
	For church planter training

Check Here	3.) How can we help you in using media? Check appropriate areas.
	Training of team members and/or national partners to become more strategic in media use and/or creation
	Strategy Development to help you develop media related methodology to reach your target group.
	Follow up design
	Consultation at AGM
	Consultation in country (if checked, when?)
	Acquire (media materials) LIST IF POSSIBLE
	Develop (research, media materials, etc) ITEMIZE
	Help in mobilizing local partners to do broad seed sowing

Check Here	4.) Do you have media materials that you have specifically developed that may not be known by others in the region? Please list below.
	5.) What are the constraints or concerns are in the local setting that prevents certain media use? (List type and mention issues)
Rate	6.) Do you have media related skills? Rate 1-10, 1 being low, 10 best
	Scriptwriting
	Audio recording
	Video shooting
	Video Editing (what program/platform?)
	Digital photography
	Photoshop
	Desktop publishing
	Web design
	Blogging
	Facebook development

Check	7.) Have you used any of the above to
	Reach your focus group
	Communicate with friends in the States

	8.) Please comment on any topic/question
	9.) Do you have any case studies where you have used media to reach your focus group that you would be willing to share?
Check	10.) Can we attribute this information to your name?
	YES
	NO

Discussion

This was sent out to about 150 Christian workers in an Asian region. We received 85 questionnaires back and identified several projects that are still continuing, one of which is discussed in Case Study - Web Comic

Written by Dan Henrich - info@comresources.org

Appendix Three:
Sample Focus Group Guide - Radio

PROJECT LIGHT BRINGER
Proposed Focus Group Discussion Guide

I. INTRODUCTION

- Mechanics of the FGD
  (Brief explanation on what an FGD is; the "house rules"; purpose of the FGD; confidentiality)
- Introduction of participants to each other
- Entertain questions from the participants

(The purpose of this portion and the Warm-up portion is to thaw-out the participants and create an atmosphere where they will be comfortable with each other.)

II. WARM-UP
Brief discussion on media habits and media consumption with emphasis on radio listenership
- When usually listen to the radio; what occasion?
- What radio station/s usually listened to?
- What time usually listen to the radio?
- What radio program/s usually listened to?
- When was the last time listen to the radio?

III. FGD PROPER

Activity 1: Listen to the Test Broadcast Material
   (**Buhi** or **Bunga)**
      (First Exposure)

Spontaneous reaction
   - Thoughts and feelings while listening
     to the test material
   - Impact and recall
   - Appeal

Activity 2: Listen Again to the Test Broadcast Material
   (**Buhi** or **Bunga**)
   (Second Exposure)

Probed Reaction on:

Appeal of Specific Elements of the proposed
   Radio Material
      – The program title
        Association with the title (Buhi nga
        Sugilanon) or (Bunga sa Bag-ong
        Kinabuhi)
        Appropriateness of the title
        Probe why/why not

      – The presentation
        Spontaneous comments
        Probe what like/ dislike about the
        presentation and why

      – Host
        Spontaneous comments
        What like/ dislike about the host and
        why

- Quality of production
What like/ dislike about the quality of production and why

Overall appeal

Activity 3: Rating of the proposed radio material as to Appeal
(Hand out Rating Scale to Each Participant)

Level of interest generated:

Propensity to listen to the program again:
- What time and how often.

Relevance/meaningfulness of the program;

Activity 4: Rating of the proposed radio material as to level of interest generated
(Hand out Rating Scale to Each Participant)

Activity 5: Listen to the Other Test Broadcast Material (**Buhi** or **Bunga**)
And Brief Discussion Only on:

Spontaneous comments
Comparison between the two
Level of interest generated
Propensity to listen to the program again:

Awareness of radio station/s which air/s religious program

What specific radio station and religious programs are these?

Readership of the Holy Bible

Attitude toward reading the Bible

IV. WRAP – UP

Any other comments / suggestions / insights to share
Thank participants and give token of appreciation.

Appendix Four: Proposal and Strategy Example

Category: Radio
Location: SouthEast Asia

This was a project proposal developed after research in the region to discover a more effective way to use short wave radio to reach a M people group.

What we were discovering is that our efforts to produce a program using contextual terminology were overwhelmed by the fact that other programmers were using more Christianized terms. Scheduling our contextualized program after a Christianized program just created problems in the understanding of the M listener.

This proposal was used as a vision statement to the Christian shortwave providers to help them understand what a MBB Block would accomplish for the Kingdom.

Vision

Believing that God is already at work touching the hearts and lives of the millions of unreached M peoples of this country, House of Life Productions is proposing the development of a comprehensive church planting strategy. This strategy uses short-wave radio as the initial tool for broad gospel seed sowing through programming we are calling the MBB Block. This block of programs is designed exclusively for M

Background Believers (MBB) and M Background Pre-Believers (MBPB) that will result in a contextual church planting movement for those outside the influence of the current church.

We are speaking to listeners in terms they can understand and trying to eliminate as much cultural impediment as possible, so that MBPB's can truly enter into God's Kingdom and demonstrate their faith in culturally relevant ways and with the necessary sensitivity to their families, culture and society.

The Medium and Results to Date

Because of the limits placed upon media in this country, short-wave radio is the perfect choice for distributing M friendly programs that sound, feel, smell, and taste pleasing to the M ear. For the past seven years, we have used a magazine style program targeting one particular language group that has found acceptance among our target audience. At the end of 4 years of programming, we have registered 1,800 members of a fan club, 600 participants in our correspondence course, 35 professions of faith through letters, and we have sold over 100 Bibles, all to a language group of less than 1 million people.

The Plan

We are now preparing to launch the same type of program in three new languages within one concentrated block of time in order to build on the previous program's success and to help listeners more easily locate our four 30-minute programs.

We have positioned the programs as pre-evangelistic. The intent is to attract listeners, enlist them in our correspondence course, answer their questions and follow up the listeners with our network of field teams, quarterly newsletters, and promotional offers.

Within the 30-minute program we use local music, M friendly greetings, text messaging response loops, short advertisements for materials, 10 to 12 minutes of dialogue on culturally appropriate topics, quizzes, birthday greetings, Bible stories, etc. to engage our listeners.

Dramatic program

As part of our strategy, we are producing a dramatic program that models for our MBB listeners how a group functions, worships, and lives together in a house church.

Our strategy has multiple integers but essentially relies upon the MBPB Block to open the door, our Correspondence Course and field teams for evangelism, and "The House of Life" drama for discipleship and church planting.

Daily program block

We are proposing daily programming in the four target languages which will be available at the beginning of April 2xxx. "The House of Life" drama is currently in post-production and is scheduled for broadcast at the beginning of March 2xxx.

In order to reach as many as possible, we desire to cross-promote our programs between the two program styles, use local newspaper ads, and also use several different broadcast providers.

Discussion

The daily programming block was approved by the broadcasters and the MPBP rolled out with a combination of already-produced contextual programming in the national language plus a minority language program.

The problem with the plan was that shortwave signals do not all reach the same area. Since our target area was large, we had to use two different transmitters and the effect of the "block" of programming was reduced.

After about a year, all program funding for the national language was withdrawn. The minority language program is continuing.

Questions

Are there any elements you can use from this proposal in other media?

Written by Dan Henrich - <u>info@comresources.org</u>

Appendix Five:
Producing Evangelistic UPG Dramas

By Carol Conkey, Create International

carol@createinternational.com

This paper originally appeared in Mediastrategy and Christian Witness by Dan Henrich

NOTE: This was written in 2000 but the approaches remain constant. A reader can learn a lot from this article.

Introduction

Create International is a frontier media ministry of Youth With A Mission. We produce both mobilization/prayer video people profiles and evangelistic audio-visual presentations to serve those working among or targeting unreached peoples. Our goal is to provide communication resources for the least evangelized mega peoples.

Audience Analysis

Obviously, a short paper cannot explain all the intricacies, research and preparation that go into each presentation. This paper will just serve as a brief explanation of some of the ways we go about developing evangelistic videos. In preparation for the project, we do various kinds of statistical and ethnographic research. We are also doing a mobilization presentation of the people at the same time so we already are doing extensive reading and research on the people for those scripts. We seek to determine factors that will make our audience listen and understand our message. Some of this research would include

1. knowing about the audience's needs
2. oral traditions
3. written traditions
4. visual perceptions
5. ethnomusicology
6. familiarity with, and previous (if any) use of multi-media.

Redemptive analogies

Missionary author Don Richardson said "God will show us what He is already doing in that culture to reveal Himself." A culture database then would be created containing information gathered through research and ethnographic interviews. This database will contain information such as indigenous concepts of God, visual symbol systems, possible redemptive analogies and other worldview perceptions. We find out about the main audience's literacy level or education. We try to obtain appealing music and good pictures appropriate to the culture. We ask many questions of field workers and our audience:

- "What are the visuals or music selections that are the most appropriate?"
- "Which ones might be misunderstood or offensive?"
-"What are appropriate costumes, gestures, visuals?"

Our normal procedure for audience analysis in all of our audio-visual presentations is as follows:

1. Prayer, asking the Lord to reveal to us keys into the peoples hearts

2. Discussions, research and questionnaires with nationals, on-field missionaries working with a particular people group

3. Pre-field and on-field library and resource gathering

4. Discussions and questionnaires with non-Christians from the target people

5. Feedback and analysis of the presentation. We have developed a three-page questionnaire that seeks to determine real and felt needs of the audience, prior knowledge of the gospel message, their view of becoming a Christian, indigenous communication, literacy level, etc. We are constantly expanding our files on people groups for each presentation. Audience analysis is key to on-going field research and then effective presentations of the gospel.

Scripting/Translation

It is usually best to have Christian nationals write the scripts in their own heart language, rather then translate the script into the heart language from English. However, there are times in our experience where this was not possible. When we did the Acehnese project in 1989, there were no known Christians in the area. We needed writers/translators who were familiar with the gospel message and how to best communicate to Muslims. However, with a team of Acehnese (Muslim) guys, we did work closely in sharing our thoughts about a script. This often led to many discussions and explanations. They would back-translate what they were writing with an Indonesian Christian to assure accuracy.

However, in most other productions we have found or worked with Christians knowledgeable in the Bible and communication who were able to write the script in the heart language and then translate the script to English for us. Usually this cannot be word for word. "Expatriates should encourage national translators and ensure they receive the necessary training to understand the Biblical background and communicate the Scriptures within a context meaningful to their own people." (Shaw, Transculturation 1988:76) When we desire to have the narration in the heart language, where it might be less spoken then the national language, we often have to have another division of translating.

It is important to have a bi-lingual helper who can communicate the message being translated to the production team. This assures us that what we intended to say is being communicated. This is especially important if we have a non-Christian translating the script. Also, sometimes translators/actors will say the script is fine and yet as they write or say their lines they change things without our knowledge. It is best to work with a team of translators to assure accuracy in translation and message content. This insures accuracy of meaning, contextualization, correct grammar and comprehension for the intended audience. It is important to learn from the translators what changes they made and why.

We have often learned some valuable ways to communicate cross-culturally, especially when trying to express complex theological concepts. In many cultures there is no single word to translate such concepts as sin, grace, redemption, salvation, and love, thus a phrase must be developed to describe it. Also, we need to be careful the translator does not simply use a word from the Bible without explanation. We need to insure that it is an understandable translation and makes sense in the heart language of the people.

We have also found in most cultures that an older man is the most respected and if that man can have the "final word" when there are negotiations, that is the best. We were fortunate that God provided such a 'man of peace' in our last project in Sumatra who was a Muslim convert, yet now a strong, mature Christian who had a balanced view of contextualization. As a film crew we often have to be aware of the cultural "hierarchy" and know who is best to communicate our thoughts to and the manner with which we should communicate to them. This often involves a layer of translations back and forth.

So we have to allow adequate time making sure there is agreement before, during and after the filming with all those who will be showing the presentation.
If all those involved feel they were heard and had input then there will be ownership of the video after it is produced. There is usually quite a lively discussion between the actors, our advisors (nationals-native speakers, on-field workers, and ourselves) so the process sometimes gets lengthy. However, our average time of shooting a 20-30 minute video is about three to four days. We do believe that we need to prepare as well as we can ahead of time, even send an advance team to go ahead of us and work out all the logistics. However, it is our experience that God has always provided the actors and participants that He has wanted in the drama, as we have trusted in Him. We do the possible and He does the impossible!

It is quite an adventure of trust, especially because we often go into areas where film crews have not been before and some of the people are often hostile to the gospel. However, a number of times we have used Muslim actors and many have expressed an interest in knowing more about the gospel. On our recent trip to Sumatra, one of the Muslim actors, a prominent traditional singer, gave his life to the Lord just after the filming and now wants to produce indigenous Christian music. God uses many ways to draw people to Himself and we want to be open to His leadings in those He wants us to have in our productions.

Field Recording

Once the script is finally approved, we number each line or phrase. We use the method of 'one or two lines at a time' for a number of reasons:

1. Our production team usually is not fluent in the language of the production, so we need to insure there are no mistakes made in filming or editing, (In all our productions so far, we have not made any mistakes because of this numbering system).

2. The actors can practice one line at a time and then act it out in a speaking manner rather then a reading style.

3. When we prepare to edit, if we don't have numbers associated with each sentence then it is just a long dialogue in an indistinguishable language and we have no point of reference for visual inserts.

4. We record and write down in phonetic lettering the first and last words of each phrase. This is helpful if we have an insert from another camera angle, add other visuals, or again as a point of reference especially in narrative sections.

5. Before each scene is done and there is a costume or location change, we go over and check to make sure no line of the script has been missed. This enables us to re-record and insert any line instead of having to do the whole translation or paragraph over.

Narration sound recording

There are advantages and disadvantages in using a sound studio on the field. If there is a sound studio available, it does insure quality and noise-free recordings. It also speeds up recording because we do not have to stop for every disruption that often takes place when recording in someone's home. However, often professional studios are not available in villages or small towns where we are doing the project. Many times we have to use any available room and put up mattresses to cushion the sound. Another advantage in doing the recording in a room, especially with a non-professional narrator, is the aspect of personal warmth and comfort to the narrator who is usually not accustomed to being behind glass in a sound booth. Often the narrator also is concerned with his security and wants to do the recording with people he knows and trusts.

We have used a Sony professional stereo Walkman cassette for past recordings. Currently we use a mini-disc digital recorder with lapel or hand-held microphone for field recording. The mini-disc recorder virtually eliminates background noise, hiss and pause "pops" and gives us excellent compressed sound quality. For many narration segments, we transfer the recordings to open reel or videotape and then take out all the numbers from the narration tape. We use our number system sheet to phonetically write out each beginning and ending word. It is a challenge for us to do all this in a largely indistinguishable language that often does not use roman lettering. It often takes quite a bit of time and effort to make sure the narration flows correctly, however, the result is usually worth the extra work. The acquired indigenous music, sound effects and other appropriate music are later added as background to the narration.

Script preparation case studies: Tibetan Buddhist

The script had to be agreed upon by over twenty workers among the Tibetan people. We knew that if everyone felt they participated in it there would be a sense of ownership and desire to use the presentation. We also highly valued each worker's contribution. However, it was quite a challenge to make everyone with different doctrinal perspectives agree. It went through about five script revisions but finally a fully approved script was produced. We had an ex-Tibetan Buddhist radio announcer as our narrator and script consultant. Through our research and interviews we found that there were several evangelistic concepts we needed to address in the script:

1. The need to show that all the "works" of Tibetan Buddhism cannot "pay for the debt". That there still existed a great need for a sacrifice by a holy being to bring us back into relationship with our Creator.

2. The power of personal experience and supernatural powers. (We were able to utilize testimonies from Tibetan believers, who freely spoke about their changed life). Jesus' power over sin, sickness, disease and demons was a dynamic redemptive key in the Tibetan worldview.

3. Compassion is also a highly valued trait. Jesus' compassion shows His tender loving care for all peoples Also His followers utilizing His compassion and prayer for others also deeply impressed the Tibetans.

4. A message such as "you must be born again" is not really appropriate in the Tibetan Buddhist worldview because they already believe in reincarnation. Instead we used the phrase, "Jesus is the liberator from the cycle of karma." This seemed to really make a positive impact on the people who viewed the presentation.

Contextualized Visualize

Great care was taken to utilize visuals which Tibetans could both identify and also understand the appropriate meaning. All visuals used in the presentation utilize actual Tibetan peoples in various aspects of their life and culture with familiar Tibetan settings. Tibetans have a piece of artwork called "The Wheel of Life" that they utilize for their religious teachings. This "Wheel of Life" (Thangka painting) depicts a demon clutching onto a wheel--portraying death and suffering with seemingly no escape. Their painting vividly depicts hopelessness.

During the pre-production scripting, we were discussing how to depict the life of Christ. Should Jesus be portrayed historically (Jew) or in robes like a monk? About a month earlier, a missionary working among the Tibetans in Nepal went to a professional Tibetan Buddhist thangka painter, gave him the Gospel of Luke and challenged him to paint what he read. What he painted, many concurred, was truly amazing. We showed this "new" thangka while on a visit to the U.S. Center for World Mission and Fuller. Many missiologists commented that this thangka painting on the life of Christ was a real "breakthrough in missiology" and missions to the Tibetans. Using a cyclical format as most Tibetan thangka paintings do, it goes through the life of Christ in meticulous detail showing the birth, miracles, teachings, Last Supper, death on the cross, burial and resurrection.

It was quite amazing that the artist depicted Christ as breaking the cycle of Karma through His resurrection. We used this painting in our video and then added dramatic effects to emphasize the release from the endless cycle of death and rebirth and to emphasize that Jesus is our Liberator from the cycle of Karma. "The endless cycle of death and rebirth which the Tibetans call the Karma chain can be a pivotal point in the Tibetans understanding, because Jesus came from outside to fulfill the Law to break the Karma chain. Instead of being blown out we are brought into a new existence, into new life. Christians can explain to

Tibetan Buddhists that the Holy Spirit sets us on the new Path towards the pure Karma--that is life in Heaven". (Interview with Passang Angmo, Tibetan Christian, 1988) We utilized many other aspects of contextualized artwork and symbols:

1. The common greeting of hands together at the chest that signify a heart greeting. I put black around the hands to symbolize darkness in the heart and then changed it to gold when the holiness of God entered the heart.

2. The white scarf is used in Tibetan practices as a sign of welcoming and blessings. We used it around the Tibetan man's neck as a sign of welcoming one into God's family and for blessing, (The white scarf has also been used in contextualized Christian baptisms).

3. When the Prodigal Son comes home, the script reads, "He caught hold of his feet..." This is a sign of deep humility and being ashamed. Also the gesture of two thumbs together and bowing down is a symbol of repentance. Our Tibetan Christian narrator told us about these gestures. We also asked the participants in the drama, "What sign would you use to show you are very sorry?" and they all immediately modeled a "two thumbs together" gesture.

Drama Participants
In advance of our coming, we had our field workers in Kathmandu set up the participants in the drama. They thought they had a Christian Tibetan family committed to participate. After we arrived, however, for a number of reasons they changed their minds and decided not to participate. There were very few other Christians in the area and even fewer men who were professing Christians. We felt God told us to go out into the Tibetan community and He would provide the participants for us.

We walked through a small town where we felt that we were to do the shooting and a Tibetan lady called out to us, "Can I help you?" in perfect English. We stopped and one of our workers shared what we needed. It just so happened she was the only one in the community that understood any English. She agreed to help us and in about 30 minutes we rounded up our whole cast, sent them home to practice their lines and to get appropriate attire and in about three days completed the shoot. We also did not know where we would shoot the drama. After a few hours of scouting, we went up to a typical Tibetan house and asked for permission to film in and around the house. They agreed and even helped us with gathering many of the needed props. We gave all the participants gifts and they seemed very happy to participate. During the filming, our missionary friends who spoke Tibetan were able to witness to the actors and house owners.

Music

Tibetan instrumental music was used throughout the presentation. An original song, sung and produced by Tibetans believers, was utilized at the end of the video.

Response from the Field

This production is probably one of our more "successful" in terms of response. Workers have excitedly been reporting that this presentation is being shown all over Northern India, Nepal, Mongolia, and China with a positive response--even among Tibetan Buddhist monks! It is still being shown at a border welcoming area and in a shop on the holy walk of Tibetans. We have been encouraged from some of the feedback: Tibetans viewing the presentation have been awed and say things like: "Jesus can really liberate me? There are other Tibetans that believe in Jesus!? How can I become a believer in this Jesus? I believe everything in this presentation." (1992 Tibetan worker's letter).

Our workers and other mission organizations have been using this presentation with very positive feedback and openness by Tibetans. Other feedback given to us that the presentation is very effective because of utilizing testimonies of Christian Tibetans, worldview shifts etc. and it is best used when the worker can personally clarify some of the points of the presentation.

Participatory script preparation case studies: Uighurs
We have developed a number of scripts suitable for showing in SE Asia and South Asia. However, even between neighboring groups we have seen quite a few adaptations needed to be made: language, clothing, cultural themes, etc. Examples of these would be, spacial dynamics related to how they conduct feasts and public events, family and gender relations, body positions and gestures, music, etc. Even in Indonesia we found we could not just do an Indonesian presentation and show it to a people group and have them feel it was tailor made for them.

Many of our presentations to Muslims we open with a 'Call to Prayer' with calligraphy and nice graphics of "Bismallah..." (The Arabic call to prayer). This is especially meaningful in presentations aimed at reaching Muslims. We focus on God-His character and greatness and leave out all references to Mohammed. Films usually open with nice scenery of the area and then focus on a man's search to know more about God. On-field missionaries wrote a good portion of the Uighur presentation. They had lived among the people for a number of years and understood the humor and really did some great contextualization. However, because they were not filmmakers they needed some adjustments from us to make it appropriate for AV. Fortunately, we were able to input quite a bit on the script via email over the course of two months and had it pretty much finalized before we arrived.

In Central Asia many of the Arts are not being funded anymore since the collapse of the Soviet Union, so professional actors are out of work. We were able to get a number of professional actors and their families to be involved in this drama and worked out a fair hourly rate. We gave them their lines a week in advance and then went away for a week to China and asked that they work on them to be ready to film when we returned. Alas we came back, for various reasons they hadn't worked on them. It seems that on every project the actors say, "If you had only given me more time I could have done better".

However most Asian societies are face-to-face cultures and no matter how soon we give the script to them it isn't until the film crew is actually there on location that much gets done. They also said "Oh, we can memorize and act out more than one line at a time!" So we said, "OK let's try it", (open for new methods) after a couple of hours however, they agreed that it was best to go one or two lines at a time. We were also in a private house setting where our video lights were draining on the houses' electricity (not to mention melting their wires). So we had the actors practice their conversation, the cultural and linguistic helpers confirmed the right words and then the lights came on and we did a few takes. We had observers from a number of agencies present so they could learn techniques for their own local A/V production center.

This Higher evangelistic video will be finished in October 1996 and then field tested. It was a good co-operative effort among a number of churches and missionaries. The team will also look at the relevance of the production for neighboring Uzbek peoples.

Several areas that we desire to improve

1. Obtaining more detailed feedback/follow-up, especially from nationals or the target people for the presentation to know how to improve the presentation. We need to ask more questions to analyze the effectiveness of these videos: "What did the video communicate to you?" "What did you think about how Jesus (or a representation) was communicated in visuals, symbols, and via the narrator?" "Would you like to know more about Jesus and the gospel message?" "What did you understand to be the message(s) of the presentation?"

2. More Distribution Statistics: How many times the field workers are showing the presentation and percentage of responses at the various levels of the evangelism process.

3. More Field Workers and Nationals to work with us on the Presentations. As the producers, we have some cultural blindness that could prevent us from knowing the right or most effective way to communicate the message. We need more advice from both believers and non-believers in our presentations. Sometimes our "point persons" are western missionaries who do not really know the best way to communicate interculturally.

4. More Time to Pretest. Sometimes we are under time constraints and do not adequately test the script and production and get feedback. We hope to have advance teams that can facilitate pre-testing. It is also good to see how/if changes have improved the program.

5. Wider distribution of these evangelistic videos for short and long term teams, television broadcast and video rental distribution. We also want to maintain the "High tech-High

touch" importance of having workers (when they can) personally discuss and follow up those viewing the presentation.

Discussion

The author has presented a very detailed guide to developing evangelistic video productions.

What elements would you include in a production you would do? Could this approach be used in an urban area? Why/ Why not?

Why do you think they have such a highly detailed approach to contextualization? Is this unique to Create International? Does Hollywood contextualize? If so, how?

www.ingramcontent.com/pod-product-compliance
Lightning Source LLC
Chambersburg PA
CBHW051212170526
45166CB00005B/1858